SUCCESS MENTALITY

SUCCESS MENTALITY

LESSONS FROM A
GEOPOLITICAL STRATEGIST

Vlada Galan

BURMAN BOOKS
MEDIA CORP.

BURMAN BOOKS
MEDIA CORP.

Published 2025 by Gildan Media LLC, aka G&D Media
by arrangement with Burman Books Media Corp.
www.GandDmedia.com

SUCCESS MENTALITY. Copyright © 2025 by Vlada Galan and
Burman Books Media Corp. All rights reserved.

No part of this book may be used, reproduced or transmitted in any manner whatsoever, by any means (electronic, photocopying, recording, or otherwise), without the prior written permission of the author, except in the case of brief quotations embodied in critical articles and reviews. No liability is assumed with respect to the use of the information contained within. Although every precaution has been taken, the author and publisher assume no liability for errors or omissions. Neither is any liability assumed for damages resulting from the use of the information contained herein.

Edited by Lara Petersen
Cover photos by Rachael Ann Gliebe
Book Design by Clarissa D'Costa

Library of Congress Cataloging-in-Publication Data is available upon request

ISBN: 978-1-7225-9919-5

10 9 8 7 6 5 4 3 2 1

This book is dedicated to my mother,

She made the sacrifice to bring me to a new country for a better life. She never quit when the going got tough.

We split every piece of bread for breakfast and walked together in the snow in sandals and socks because we had no other shoes.

I will never forget the journey. This was all for you. You are my purpose.

Mom, may you never forget us—the two poor immigrants who arrived in Los Angeles with a cardboard sign in September 1996.

We have made them proud.

CONTENTS

1. EVERYTHING YOU NEED IS WITHIN YOURSELF 9
2. WHAT DO YOU ACTUALLY WANT? 39
3. BELIEVE YOU ARE WORTHY 69
4. STOP DREAMING AND START WORKING—THE PLAN 87
5. DROPPING DEAD WEIGHT 107
6. ELIMINATING DISTRACTIONS 137
7. EXECUTION IS KEY 157
8. FIGURE IT OUT 173
9. "NO" IS NOT AN ANSWER 193
10. ALL IS FAIR IN LOVE AND WAR 209
11. STOP MAKING EASY DECISIONS 231
12. THE TABLE 247
13. DEMAND MORE IN LIFE 265

CHAPTER 1
─────────

EVERYTHING YOU NEED IS WITHIN YOURSELF

Life is a funny thing. We constantly seek something outside of ourselves—validation from others or admiration from people who have done less than us, without realizing the powerhouse is within us. Is it so shocking that it's our qualities and DNA that make us unique? Generations before you had to survive so you could be here right now. That isn't an accident; it reflects a strong line of succession. Whether you come from a complicated background or a successful one, that isn't what defines you. You must define yourself, live by your own rules, and tap into the powerhouse that you are.

You need to activate your bloodline of success. While you can mimic anyone, you are the only one who can be your original self. What makes you unique is that no one can be you or do what you do. So why settle for being a copy? Why not choose to be the original—exactly who you are?

Perhaps you feel this way because you aren't confident in exactly who you are, or maybe you're confident in many aspects, like I was, yet there remains that nagging doubt. You may have that little voice whispering that you aren't good enough, don't have what it takes, or don't deserve a seat at the table. Maybe you don't know how to demand a place at the table, or you've forgotten that you can build your own table and decide who sits at it with you.

I'm going to help you silence that voice in your head, and you're going to activate the most extraordinary success formula in your life. You didn't get here by accident; you have always been destined for more. You are not going to let down the generations who persevered before you. It's all too easy to say, "I come from nothing; I will never amount to anything," or to get lazy and fall back on a strong, successful family member. If you're looking for the easy button, it doesn't exist. You won't screw this up. Instead, you're going to toughen up, get it together, and get more out of life than you ever thought possible.

I will teach you the steps to achieve more, demand more, and change your mindset and habits. Once we're done here, you'll be conquering the world one day at a time. I won't accept anything less, and neither will you.

It was a cold, snowy day in Russia, September 1996. My frosty golden locks bounced off the collar of my red wool coat. We began in Odesa, Ukraine, and had arrived in Moscow to continue our journey. If ever there was a day when I felt nervous, scared, and didn't believe in myself, it was that day. I was just six years old.

That was the day I met doubt, fear, and the unknown. You know the day I'm talking about—everyone remembers the day they first faced doubt and uncertainty head-on. My life was about to change forever as I boarded a Boeing 747 with my mother. I said goodbye to my grandma, the truest love I had ever known, as we prepared to fly to a foreign land: America, specifically Los Angeles. I didn't know whether I would ever see my grandma or my dad again. I was truly facing the unknown.

I felt a warm hand take mine—my mother's small hand intertwined with mine. "It's time," she said. Tears streamed down my cheeks as I looked back at my grandma. Upon seeing her expression, I knew change would be scary and uncomfortable. I was saying goodbye to everything I knew, including that scared little Ukrainian girl inside me.

On that long transatlantic flight to the new world, I dug deep and realized that, even if I didn't want to face the unknown, I had no choice. We had no money and no grand plan, but my mother knew she wanted more out of life. She had taken a big step—one that would define my life forever.

On the plane, I asked, "*Mamochka*, how will I learn English? How will I make new friends? How will I get to a new school?"

She smiled, but I could see the doubt in her eyes. I sensed her uneasiness. "Everything you need is within yourself," she stated firmly, tapping my chest. "God put it there. Your will is powerful enough to blaze any trail you want."

Everything you need is within yourself.

I will remember those words forever, and now, so will you.

We landed in sunny California, holding a cardboard sign bearing the name of the family we were there to meet. We settled in slowly and were provided with accommodation until we could make a plan.

The dreaded day came when I had to go to a new school, River Canyon Elementary. The students greeted me, and all I could say was "hello" and "elephant"—those were the only two words I knew. "Everything you need is within you," I reminded myself. The first days of school were easy, and quite honestly, a blur.

In the third week of school, the class was doing a reading assignment, and I couldn't participate since I didn't know how to read in English. The students all sat with their desks arranged in a circle, while I was segregated in the corner like an outcast. I felt embarrassed and flushed with humiliation. Why wasn't I part of the circle? I heard whispers as students made fun of me and I realized I had two choices: 1) allow this to define me, or 2) create my own destiny.

With my heart racing a million miles a minute, I slowly stood up. The reading circle fell silent. I dragged my desk to the middle of the room, breaking the circle and put my desk smack dab in the middle of it. If they wanted to talk about me, I was going to give them something to talk about. No one would put me in a corner.

That day, I discovered one of my strengths: courage. The teacher didn't say a word, and my classmates stared in shock at the girl who dared to define herself. The teacher came over, pronounced the words on the page, and I repeated them. She smiled and patted my back. "Good job," she said. I was in! I became part of the circle because I had found courage.

That lesson has never left me. Each of us can recall and reflect on the lessons that revealed our strengths. Perhaps you didn't even realize it at the time. Together, we are going to discover your strengths and weaknesses, and then weaponize them to make you a winning machine. The best part is that you already possess all the strengths you need to be successful. You just don't know it yet. You have probably been on a quest, searching for something outside of yourself, or you've been looking in the wrong place. Let's dig in.

I. YOUR ASSETS

Not understanding your strengths and abilities can lead to many challenges in life. The work we are beginning together requires you to start with the foundation. This is where you discover what you're made of. I cannot take you places if you don't first take the time to recognize which tools in your toolbox will help you get there. Failing to understand your strengths and assets has some serious negative consequences. If you don't know what skills you possess, then you have no idea what you're good at or could excel in within your career and personal life, nor will you recognize opportunities that align with your natural skill set.

This leads to finding yourself in a worthless dead-end job. Worse yet, it can create a false belief that you can't do anything right at work, when in reality, you're just not in the right place to succeed because you aren't focusing on what you're better suited for. This blind spot will cause you to have self-doubt, undermine your confidence and performance, and affect how you portray yourself.

When you don't understand your strengths, how can you know what to focus on? Conversely, if you know where your talents lie, focusing on those areas will yield the best long-term results, making you a more accomplished individual in the long run. When you know your strengths and skill set, you become an unstoppable force because you don't have to rely on anyone. What you need is deep within you.

Knowing how to leverage your strengths will maximize your potential by allowing you to improve those areas. When you know what you're good at, you make better decisions in both your career and personal life because you can match your strengths to the paths that are best for you.

At work, this will pay dividends. Everyone will notice your prowess when you focus on your strengths, which will open doors to new opportunities.

You may be wondering where to start. First, you need to understand what kind of thinker you are. We begin by understanding whether you're more math-oriented or more inclined toward social sciences and creative thinking. If you excelled in math-related subjects, you're likely a linear thinker, meaning your thought process moves in a straight line, allowing you to deliver information in perfect order from start to finish. You draw on past experiences to make conclusions and look for patterns and consistency. If you can sit down and complete a task from start to finish in one sitting, you're a linear thinker.

On the other hand, if you're a more creative individual and catch yourself thinking ahead rather than taking things step by step, you're a lateral thinker. You look at situations from various perspectives. Your thinking may appear disorganized, but this allows you to be more innovative and come up with new ideas easily.

If you are a linear thinker, your strengths will naturally lie in organization and streamlining processes. You excel in attention to detail, clear communication, result-oriented tasks, and anticipating problems before they arise. If this describes you, embrace opportunities to take on projects and lead them. You are the ideal candidate to meet deadlines, get organized, and manage a team.

As you continue on the journey of embracing a success mentality, you'll realize that you excel at making and executing a plan. Your ability to foresee potential problems will help you avoid common mistakes. I admire linear thinkers and their organizational skills. My husband is an excellent example of a linear thinker.

If you're a lateral thinker, you're innovative and willing to take risks. Overly rigid structures won't suit you, and you'll always question the status quo. You can encourage everyone around you to think in new directions, which means you should feel empowered to speak up in group settings. Your open-minded approach makes you an asset to any organization. Lateral thinkers can't be confined to a box. You're the perfect person for brainstorming sessions. As we further embrace the success mentality, you'll realize that you excel at dreaming up big ideas and discovering shortcuts to get there. You are always adapting as you go. I understand this well because I'm a lateral thinker.

Now that you have a basic understanding of your thinking style, let's look at your other strengths and how you can leverage them. You may perceive some of these traits as negative, but I will show you why what others think are your worst qualities can be your greatest assets. You may not possess all these traits; instead, focus on the ones that resonate with you most and work on enhancing them.

Emotional IQ is the ability to read the room and the people around you while maintaining self-awareness in all situations. This kind of emotional intellect allows you to build and maintain healthy relationships and navigate various situations with ease. Not everyone has a high emotional IQ, but if you do, you may be taking this strength for granted. Emotionally intelligent people know how to read other people very well. They sense when someone is happy or sad and can effectively navigate their own emotions. Use your emotional IQ to regulate your emotions in stressful situations and gauge other people's emotions. I have a high emotional IQ, and when I'm closing a deal with a client, I sense their hesitation. I focus on it and address their fears or insecurities directly. If I sense they're overwhelmed, I step back and let go of the situation, careful not to overplay my hand.

Impatience is your unwillingness to wait. Embrace it and apologize to no one. This is a true strength. Impatience drives you to push for faster results and higher productivity than those around you. Impatient people are much quicker at making decisions, adapting, and advocating for change. Impatience is an engine that will drive you farther in life. I can't tell you how many times I've been labeled impatient. I used to feel like I needed to be more restrained and keep it under control. When I recalibrated my thinking to embrace a success mindset, I realized impatience suited my competitive nature perfectly. When I embraced it, I saw real results.

Courage is the ability to face fear and the unknown and tackle it head-on. This is your ability to push past your fears and move forward. It's a strength you can develop, so even if you don't have it, you can cultivate it by putting yourself in uncomfortable situations that force you to face your fears. I used to have a fear of public speaking, which I laugh at now. In one of my jobs, I forced myself to take on the role of speaking at events. It was terrifying at first, but I pushed through. Over time, taking on things I feared became easier. Cultivating this skill will serve you well.

Humility is your ability to be modest instead of arrogant and overly prideful. Although you may be the quietest person in the room who doesn't seek glory to stroke your ego, you're not to be disregarded. You'll always be underestimated, and this makes you the silent killer. While everyone is trotting around, gloating, or boasting, you're learning and developing faster than others. This ability to stay grounded allows you to be strategic. I don't possess this skill, but I have learned so much from those who do. They come out of nowhere and get ahead by remaining in the background and moving in silence. If humility is your strength, you may often be underestimated, but don't let it bother you. Instead, bide your time and strike when the time is right. Your secret weapon is being underestimated.

Confidence is your ability to believe in yourself. It isn't thinking you're better than everyone else, rather, it's realizing you have no reason to compare yourself to others. We've all struggled with self-doubt at various points in our lives. This strength can be developed, but it requires practice. No one woke up one day believing they were the best at everything. Confidence is important because it allows you to believe in yourself and your abilities enough to take risks, which leads to personal growth. Confidence is an asset, but be careful not to over-inflate yourself, or it will be your biggest downfall. Ego kills more dreams than you realize, so check yours at the door.

Aggressiveness is characterized by having a forceful and dominant attitude. Many career-driven women are labeled as such. Embrace it. Working in a man's world, I quickly learned that being aggressive is necessary, and while men may not agree, it ultimately isn't a negative trait. Aggressiveness makes you assertive, determined, competitive, and an incredibly strong negotiator. If you're aggressive, you'll work well in high-pressure environments.

Great leaders often exhibit this trait. If this describes you, you're destined to lead.

These are some key strengths vital for success, but you don't need to possess all of them. Even if you embody just one of these strengths, you've got a solid foundation to build upon. You can always develop more strengths as you go; however, before you get too far ahead, I must warn you that you will encounter imposter syndrome. This is why you must understand your thinking style and what strengths you have. This knowledge allows you to tackle imposter syndrome.

II. IMPOSTER SYNDROME

Part of the problem of not understanding your strengths and weaknesses is the deep-seated belief that you don't have what it takes. This mentality inevitably leads to imposter syndrome. Let me tell you something, and you'd better listen up—no matter how confident you believe yourself to be, or how good you think you are, don't lie to yourself while reading this. Don't believe for one second that this isn't me talking to you about *you*. Imposter syndrome affects everyone at some point or another. I'm overly confident in many aspects of my life, but I have also grappled with imposter syndrome. It's real, and it affects everyone.

We've all stood in a room and thought, "I don't belong here. I'm not like the rest of these people. They're smarter, more educated, wealthier, and prettier than me." The list goes on. Well, I am here to tell you that voice belongs to the frightened "loser child" within you. We all have one. Loser sounds awful, but it deserves recognition for what it is. If left unchecked, imposter syndrome brings out the inner loser. Do not allow this to happen; without intervention, it can trigger a real spiral that will send you down a path that alters your future. You must stop imposter syndrome dead in its tracks.

My life has been full of imposter syndrome moments, which I call my "loser moments." Years ago, when I was attending university, I worked full time in various managerial roles at the biggest bar and club in the city. At one point, I launched the corporate events department, leasing the space to Fortune 500 companies for private events. With a full salary and commission, I was earning double the national average income, and I was just twenty-three years old. I was making more money than people with multiple college degrees. My car was paid off, and I had a two-storey apartment right next to the university. I was debt-free and paid my tuition out of pocket. I was proud of myself because I had done it all on my own. I didn't have a rich daddy to fall back on or a trust fund, just a strong mindset. Thanks to my mom, I knew hard work would get me there.

I was beyond confident in the hospitality industry. I could walk into any bar or restaurant and get a free meal or drink because everyone knew I was a manager at a top club in the city. Confidence wasn't lacking, to say the least. As graduation approached, I wanted to start my career in the world of politics. It meant leaving a high-paying job to make peanuts working on political campaigns. Talk about a change of environment.

The change was daunting. I traded miniskirts and platinum blonde hair for business suits and darker hair so I'd be taken seriously. After volunteering on a political campaign, I looked for an opportunity to start working on one. In my state, there was a huge election wave, and I was offered a position working for a powerful legislator from the Georgia General Assembly. He was the majority whip, which is a leadership position in the ruling party. The majority whip is an important figure in the political game who helps the party stay united and get votes behind key legislative bills. In short, he was a big deal with some big names and big money behind his bid to run for United States Congress.

I joined the campaign and couldn't have been more excited. It took me all of three days to figure out that what they taught me in college was no preparation for real-life work experience in my chosen career. So, what to do? I knew I'd have to learn fast and blaze a trail, and blaze a trail I did, but not without facing imposter syndrome. It strikes you right in the face most often when you're daring to step out of your comfort zone or desperately trying to take the next step to become a better version of yourself.

To start my career, I took a massive salary cut and had to reinvent myself. I went on a mad shopping spree to replace my wardrobe, colored my hair a darker tone, and got ready to dive headfirst into politics. The campaign office was my new classroom. I read a lot and worked on as many things as I could to expand my skill set.

I tried to prove myself worthy of being there. I wanted to be the absolute best. We often try so hard because we don't believe we are the best. I realized I was really good—better than half the people I worked with—until doubt and fear crept in.

The essential part of any political campaign is raising money, and our candidate was the most connected out of all the candidates. He had just about every state legislator and senator in the state on his side. I was asked to support the fundraising team at a huge event at a private club, which was a big deal. It was *the* event of the month. State legislators, senators, and the who's who of politics would be there. I bought a new dress for the occasion and was excited to collect checks and shake down some wealthy donors.

It was a happy hour-type event with drinks and hors d'oeuvres. I arrived at the city club and immediately felt flush. I stood helplessly in front of the building. "What am I doing here?" I asked myself. Thoughts raced through my mind. A private city club? "You're just a poor Ukrainian girl. You've never been to a private club. You don't belong here."

The sinking feeling grew. Walking into the southern good ol' boys' club was overwhelming. Most guests were wealthy southern American elites. I was no one. They'd see right through me. I was shaking. Just like that, imposter syndrome struck me in the face. I felt like a loser in a nice dress, but I kept it together, realizing that no matter how much I wanted to run away and be a real loser, I needed to dig deep and get my head in the game.

"Deal with these emotions later," I told myself. "Right now, you must be here for your job, so suck it up." I flung the door open and walked in with a demanding, albeit insecure, presence. The staff sensed my unease. "I'm here for a fundraising event," I mumbled. The staff directed me to the elevators, and as I rode up, imposter syndrome ate me alive.

The elevator doors opened, and I made my way to the event room. I heard roaring laughter all the way down the hall. Panic set in as I entered the room. I wasn't one of them, and I didn't belong. Until that point, I'd been doing well in my job, and my confidence was at an all-time high. I'd received a huge promotion and was more than capable of doing the work. So why did I suddenly feel like I didn't belong?

Imposter syndrome is funny that way. None of the facts matter. It just takes over and makes you feel inferior.

I frantically looked around the room to find a face I recognized: the campaign manager. I slapped on a cheerful smile before speaking with him. "Why are you talking to me?" he asked. "You should be talking to donors."

Just like that, the security blanket was gone. For a moment, I stood there dumbstruck before making my way to the bar for a glass of wine. I approached a group of men and women in deep conversation, hoping to casually insert myself, but to them, I was invisible. They didn't even acknowledge my presence. I felt even more defeated, so I moved on.

Eventually, I struck up a conversation with a legislator who asked about my background. He seemed genuinely interested in talking to me, amazed by my story and the fact that I spoke a second language, and showed interest in my thoughts on government issues. We chatted for a while before he handed me a check for the fundraiser. I was ecstatic and realized I wasn't a loser after all. In fact, I had overcome more challenges than most of the people in that room.

I told myself that no matter how uncomfortable a situation became, I'd make my way around the room and make myself known. I wouldn't cower and hide in the back because of some loser thoughts swirling in my mind. Not me. I affirmed that I belonged there. I pushed my way into every conversation that evening, even approaching the group by the bar that had previously ignored me. If they didn't want to acknowledge me, I simply introduced myself and extended my hand for a handshake. I didn't care if it felt humiliating. I was no loser, and I wouldn't let imposter syndrome ruin me—not that day, not ever.

I share this story to emphasize that no matter how confident you are, imposter syndrome will affect you at some point. It's critical to understand where it comes from. Mine stemmed from my background as a poor immigrant. That day, I identified it, although that wasn't the first time I'd faced it.

Where does your imposter syndrome stem from? Is it linked to insecurities about your background, physical appearance, education, financial situation, or skill set? Right now, I want you to take a long, deep pause and reflect on the last time you experienced imposter syndrome. Be honest with yourself: what triggered it? How did you handle it? Did you let it overwhelm you, or did you confront it?

The next time this happens, I want you to follow these golden rules—the three A's:

Affirm

Stop the minute imposter syndrome strikes and start the affirmation process. Say these words to yourself: "I am not a loser. I have what it takes, and I'm here for a reason. I belong here, I have a unique skill set, and I'm going to finish what I started. I am the best."

Accept

Accept and acknowledge your feelings. If you feel like you don't belong, ask yourself why. Acceptance is the first step toward a solution. Once you get to the root of your feelings, accept the revelation, but for the time being, put it in a mental box. In the moment—especially in public—is not the time to work through it. Acknowledge the feeling, but now you must act.

Act

Taking action is always the hardest part. No matter how uncomfortable it was for me, I didn't run away; I walked into the room. You must do the same. Acting means pushing yourself out of what feels safe and comfortable, and putting on an almost-fake arrogance to take the bull by its horns and do it.

I promise you that, after following these three steps, you'll approach imposter syndrome differently. These steps will force you to psych yourself up to believe you can succeed. Identify the root cause and then get your act together. What these steps don't allow you to do is be a loser—staying down and hiding. So, anytime you face imposter syndrome, remember to Affirm, Accept, and Act. You'll thank me later. That will be the last time you allow imposter syndrome to affect critical life moments. The secret is: the more you overcome it, the less it rears its ugly head. That's because you're addressing its core.

Most of the time, the root of imposter syndrome is not believing in yourself or your strengths. Get on top of it and start believing in yourself.

III. BELIEVE IN YOURSELF AND YOUR STRENGTHS

The hardest thing to do is to believe in yourself. It's quite pathetic, but it's true. Not believing in yourself doesn't mean you don't have the skill set or inner strength; it means you haven't learned how to put all these parts together to make them work in harmony. Many times, you have all the ingredients, yet you don't end up with the finished product. That's because it requires a recipe. The ingredients must be combined in a certain way to yield a successful outcome. What others perceive as negatives about you can always be leveraged to achieve something positive at the right time.

Everything has a time and place. Learn when and where to apply your strengths and weaknesses. You'll quickly learn that you have a few weaknesses. When harnessed the right way and at the right time, they're all strengths. This is the power of mastering yourself. Having a negative quality is subjective; what one person sees as negative, another might view differently. Properly channeling these aspects can transform them into a weapon that can empower you in ways you can't even imagine.

Learn to read the room so you can tailor your approach in real time in any environment. That's why emotional IQ is so important. Reading these situations gives you clues about which tools to use.

In negotiations, it's always better to be underestimated. Often, in these environments, you need to learn to play dumb, ask a lot of questions, and be humble. Let others think you don't know what you're talking about before you go in for the kill.

In other situations, overconfidence is necessary for someone to buy into you and what you're selling. Being humble doesn't help here. Sometimes you need to allow your negative traits to shine, such as being aggressive. I can become aggressive in situations that don't seem to be going my way. For years, I was told to control myself, get a grip, settle down, and approach things more calmly. I believed I had to manage this negative aspect of my personality; however, I learned that everything I have within myself is there for a reason. We just need to learn when and where to apply our various characteristics.

After working in the international political arena for a few years, I had the opportunity to work in Africa. I couldn't have been more excited to work on my first African presidential campaign. It was a significant learning curve. I faced backlash for my American approach to work, as people felt I was too demanding and straightforward. They wanted the kiss-ass approach. I understood that I was a foreigner in their country, and my approach was different, but I was there to win an election in three months. I plowed through the election without making many friends. I questioned my own aggressive nature, but Africans are strong, incredible people who overcome more daily challenges than any of us can imagine. I realized that only the strong survive in Africa.

After winning my first African presidential election, I was exhausted from feeling like no matter what I did, it wasn't perceived well. I moved on to work in other countries in the southern African region, taking on various types of government relations projects. I tried harder to be more respectful, less demanding, and approach things as professionally as possible. Well, guess what . . . it got me nowhere. Africans are strong, and if you want to survive in a world dominated by strength, you'd better prove that you have what it takes to play their game.

I had just closed a million-dollar contract for the year with an amazing southern African country. I met the president and foreign minister, and was looking forward to getting started. Upon flying home after signing the contract, my business partner informed me that the government signed the exact same contract with a competing firm. I was in shock. In fact, the government had signed their contract before mine. Given the nature of the work, it's not customary to have two companies doing the work, and it would never succeed. When I made calls, no one seemed to know any details about the other contract. They said we must start the work and that they would address it themselves, as needed.

I began working tirelessly on the project, establishing a huge team of former congressmen and senators to support the project. The first month came and went, and so did the second and third, yet no payments had been made to our firm. I had played nice and been patient, but I was growing angry with the situation. It was unacceptable.

I visited the head of the national bank, who was supposed to issue the wire. He played nice and told me all the right things, yet nothing was done. I realized another skill set was needed here. The anger took over, along with my aggressive nature. Instead of suppressing that angry, aggressive woman, I let her out and showed everyone what she was made of.

I documented all my payment requests and analyzed the pattern of what seemed to be a game being played. The government had issued the pay order, but the head of the national bank was delaying it for personal reasons. I realized I would have to unleash my fury. Every time a lie emerged about the payment, I recorded it and sent it to all relevant parties. This became an embarrassing game for the bank governor; he was livid. Who was I, some young woman making him look bad? I became persistent to a degree I didn't know I was capable of. With nonstop texts and calls, I increased the pressure daily. I eventually went directly to the president to address the issue.

At last, I could see cracks in the foundation. My aggressive persistence seemed to be working, because I received a payment confirmation. Imagine my shock and dismay when the wire confirmation turned out to be fake. He had outplayed me. Now it was personal. My aggression was going to go full force. I sent him a text stating that a fake wire confirmation was unacceptable.

Imagine a female consultant in a male-dominated field going head-to-head with an African male, one of the most influential and well-known figures in his country. It was unheard of, and probably quite stupid. I didn't care; they had unleashed the dragon. I would not accept being lied to. He responded to my message, shaming me and asking me how I dared to accuse him of such a horrible thing. I stood my ground and maintained my aggression.

I didn't stop there. Refusing to stay silent, I went to anyone in a position of power who'd listen, sharing the messages and fake documents. In the end, they processed the full payment, and payments were never late again. In fact, something magical happened: we became close friends. It took some time to realize it had been an initiation game of sorts. They wanted to know what I was made of. My aggressive nature was my best asset. They realized

I was resilient, and if they couldn't beat me and kick me out of the country, they had to join me, pay me, and let me do my work.

That day, I discovered that what others considered my weaknesses was actually one of my greatest assets. The running joke became, "Don't make Vlada mad; she'll come for you." I smile every time I hear that. I demonstrated that I was no pushover, and I embraced a quality I didn't know was an asset. Society has trained us to believe aggression in women is wrong, but it certainly isn't.

The key lesson is that I believed in myself enough to go full force. Sometimes that's what it takes. I didn't have much to lose, so I gave it my all. Of course, I had to take a risk, but the benefits often outweigh the cost. Most of the time it works out, so why not go for it?

What qualities of yours have others labeled as negative? What people often perceive as negative traits can actually be some of the strongest qualities successful people possess because they know how to use them. Powerful people can smell weakness from a mile away. When you embrace your "negative" traits, people realize you're not afraid. You stand in your own power. Power attracts power and teaches people how to approach you. In the end, they will respect you more and want you on their team.

CHAPTER ONE LESSONS

Life often leads us to seek validation from others instead of recognizing our inherent power. The strength to succeed lies within each of us, shaped by our unique backgrounds. Regardless of where we come from, we have the ability to define ourselves and achieve our goals by embracing our individuality.

1. Self-Recognition

Your uniqueness stems from your qualities and DNA. They carry the legacy of generations before you. Recognize and embrace this because it is crucial for activating your potential for success.

2. Originality Over Imitation

Instead of copying others, strive to embrace your original self. Confidence is vital, as self-doubt will prevent you from claiming your rightful place.

3. Overcoming Doubt and Fear

Accepting that fear is part of the journey is essential. Everyone faces moments of fear and uncertainty, but it's your choice to succumb to it or to confront those feelings.

4. The Power of Self-Motivation

Personal growth comes from within. You must acknowledge your own capabilities and work toward self-improvement, regardless of your starting point.

5. Understanding Personal Strengths

Recognizing your strengths and weaknesses is critical. This self-awareness leads to better career decisions and helps avoid stagnation.

6. Types of Thinkers

Understanding whether you're a linear or lateral thinker can guide you in harnessing your strengths effectively:

- Linear Thinkers: organized, detail-oriented, and methodical.
- Lateral Thinkers: innovative, creative, and adaptable.

7. Recognizing Your Strengths

Everyone has unique strengths, including emotional intelligence, impatience, courage, humility, confidence, and aggressiveness. Leveraging these traits can propel you forward.

8. Addressing Imposter Syndrome

Imposter syndrome is common, leading to feelings of not belonging or inadequacy. Tackle it by following the three-step approach: Affirm your worth, Accept your feelings, and Act on them.

9. Believing in Yourself

Self-belief is crucial. It's about knowing how to utilize your qualities effectively. Channeling perceived negative traits as strengths can be transformational.

Our innate qualities—even those deemed negative—can be powerful assets when harnessed correctly. By understanding and embracing yourself, you can conquer challenges and achieve your goals. Believing in your strengths is key to navigating life's challenges and making an impactful presence in the world. Embrace your uniqueness and let it guide you toward success.

CHAPTER ONE EXERCISE

Identifying Your Strengths and Weaknesses

Write down your strengths.

Write down your weaknesses.

How can you use your strengths to your advantage in your environment?

How can you leverage your weaknesses to your advantage?

Assess whether you're a linear or lateral thinker.

- **Linear thinker**: focused on organization and streamlining processes. Your strengths include attention to detail, clear communication skills, results orientation, and the ability to foresee problems before they arise.
- **Lateral thinker**: innovative thinker and inclined to take risks. You may struggle in overly rigid structures. You consistently question the status quo and your thought process resembles a zigzag pattern rather than a straight line.

Now that you know what kind of thinker you are, identify the types of roles you can take on in your work environment.

CHAPTER 2

WHAT DO YOU ACTUALLY WANT?

The million-dollar question is: what do you actually want in life? The reality is that you probably have no idea. You think you know, but when asked, you hesitate because you truly don't. So, if you don't have a clear destination, how on earth do you plan on getting there?

If you don't know what you want, you can't possibly know how to get it, which means you're aimlessly living day to day—going through the motions of waking up, working, and repeating. What's it all for? Clearly, it's not for you—you're merely surviving. Getting by day-to-day is survival mode, so snap out of it. That's not the recipe for success. Dream big and have a vision. Go big or go home. Stop surviving and start thriving. Let's build your vision and understand what you actually want.

By the end of my first two years working in the political arena, I had worked on a US congressional race and a US Senate race, and wrapped up the campaign season with a winning governor's race in my home state. I was on top of the world, so why was I sitting on my couch eating a six-pack of doughnuts every day? The answer was simple: I had no vision. There I was, finishing the campaign cycle with immense success and experience, launching my career to the next level, and yet I had no idea what I actually wanted. When you don't have a vision and don't know what you want, you become bored, lazy, and lifeless. I was gaining weight and watching stupid reality TV shows, and had no clue where to go next. I was going nowhere.

I finally got off the couch and started working out, but it didn't help much. Your weight won't budge until you have a broader purpose in life. At least, that was the case for me. I couldn't shake the rut I was in, so I reached out to contacts to consider my next career move. I wanted to move to Washington, DC, and work on Capitol Hill. A new senator from our state had just been elected to the United States Senate. I knew his team and had briefly worked with them. I reached out, and he brought me in for an interview. They were hiring—how exciting!

Dan, who had led the campaign, interviewed me. He asked what position I wanted, and I shot for a decent mid-level position. With a chuckle, Dan said, "That's a pretty senior role, don't you think?"

I was appalled, because it really wasn't. Did this guy think I'd take an entry-level, carry-your-bags-around job? No thanks! Dan said they'd get back to me, but I wasn't feeling very hopeful.

Weeks went by, and there was no word. By that point, I was crashing with my friend in Washington, DC, interviewing for various jobs. The positions were scattered across the spectrum of political work. My friend, who was a true Washington insider, got me a meeting with someone in my area of expertise. The meeting was a blur, but one thing that stood out was the question: "What do you actually want to do? It seems like you're applying for anything and everything, but have no idea what you truly want." She was right. It stung! I lacked vision and a grand plan. I didn't even have a five-year plan, much less a ten-year plan. I was a grown-up who couldn't grow up.

That night, as I stared at the US Capitol building in the distance while trying to fall asleep on my girlfriend's couch, I asked myself: what does Vlada want? I told myself the sky is the limit. If I could have anything, what would it be? Removing the limitations of what was feasible shifted my perspective. Right there and then, I realized I wanted to be a millionaire. I wanted to buy my mom a house and a car, and eventually enable her to retire as a way to thank her for all the sacrifices she made for me as a single mother coming to a new country. Professionally, I wanted respect in the political sphere, a chance to change the world, and to empower people who would make a difference. Personally, I wanted to travel the world and marry someone successful. Suddenly, I wanted the world, and I wasn't going to stop until I got it.

I realized that, for twenty-five years, I had been too scared to even consider what I wanted because it seemed unattainable, so I shied away from thinking big. That night, I asked myself why I couldn't have the things I wanted. How did successful people get what they wanted? They didn't settle for less—that's how. They didn't think small. Instead, they had a vision and put in the work. I realized I didn't have to know the "how" to understand the "what" or the "why."

A funny thing happens when you dare to dream big: you become different. You start to see a clearer picture in the distance. I woke up the next day feeling transformed. That day, I got my diet in order and started approaching meetings differently. I had no idea how I was going to become a millionaire or change the world, but I knew it wouldn't happen while eating doughnuts on the sofa.

I knew that working as a senator's aide for peanuts wouldn't do it either, so I stopped applying for jobs that didn't match my experience. Now that I knew what I wanted, I attended interviews differently. I may not have known the pathway to my goal, but I knew what didn't align with my goal.

When you dare to dream and put forth your vision, you naturally begin letting go of what doesn't fit into that picture. I didn't know exactly what would get me there, but I wasn't shy about rejecting what wouldn't. It doesn't take a rocket scientist to figure out that working a dead-end job just to put working in Washington, DC, on the résumé doesn't get you places. It didn't take long for the universe to answer me. I didn't get the job for the senator, or even the second senator who interviewed me, and I thanked the universe for it. Why? Because rejection is redirection. It was the divine telling me that those opportunities weren't part of my mission.

From that day forward, my life changed. I viewed everything through the lens of "Does this match what I want?" At last, I knew what I wanted. I started dressing like a millionaire, speaking like I was accomplished, and accepting nothing less than that vision. I reached out to successful people I knew to pick their brains about work, life, and success. I can't explain it, but my life felt guided by a vision. So, how did I arrive at that vision?

I. THE "WHY"

Deep down inside, all of us have something that makes us tick. Often, we don't know where to look for it or how to identify it. Your "why" is your sense of purpose—your daily driver that pushes you to seek more in life. If you don't know your "why," we need to identify it because, without it, the journey to success is meaningless. Without your "why," you'll struggle to find fulfillment and won't see any meaning in your goals. You must know what matters to you and why you're on this earth. At this stage in life, you're in self-discovery mode. Together, we will identify your "why."

You may think I'm some mad genius who, in the middle of the night on some couch in Washington, DC, put her life into perspective and discovered her vision, but it wasn't as simple as that. I'm not a mad genius; I simply realized something that night—my "why."

I gained clarity by first thinking of the people in my life who mattered. Thinking small is an insult to the people in my life who sacrificed literally everything to help me succeed, and yet I considered some staff assistant jobs when I had two years of serious experience and a track record of success.

My "why" was my family. My mom was reason number one, and my grandparents, who had just immigrated to the USA, were reason number two. How could I be so selfish? Who was going to take care of them? That night on my girlfriend's sofa sparked my admission of what I truly wanted. I figured out my "why" in life. It was me. I knew I deserved more out of this life. I was living my youth, and I needed to make those years worthwhile.

Start with some internal reflection by first assessing what you care about most and what you're passionate about. Look deeper into your values, which define you. The core tenants of your "why" are:
- Fulfillment
- Core Values
- Passion

Your "why" exists at the intersection of these three points: what fulfills you, what you're passionate about, and what touches on your core values.

Figuring out your "why" changes everything. Is it your family, or something more selfish than that? Maybe it stems from the suffering you've experienced in life, and you refuse to let your past define you. Perhaps you need to prove something to someone. Everyone's "why" is different. So, what's yours?

You can start by answering these five questions:
1. Are you happy with where you are in life?
2. Do you feel you deserve more out of life?
3. Who matters more to you than anyone else in the world?
4. Who do you want to see you succeed more than anyone else?
5. What do you want to prove more than anything else in life?

These may seem like simple questions, but their answers yield a wealth of information that will help you identify your "why."

- If you're not happy with where you are in life, change it.
- If you feel you deserve more out of life, go get it.
- If someone means the world to you, that makes them part of your "why."
- If you want to prove something to yourself or others, that's also part of your "why."

Simply put, the main reason should always be because YOU DESERVE MORE. The rest is supplemental to that cause.

For me, I knew I wasn't happy in life and that I deserved more. My mom was counting on me to succeed and I wanted to prove, first and foremost, to myself that I could do it. The rejection from multiple jobs made me want to prove to everyone that, in a few years, I would be light-years ahead of them.

Deep down, I always had a "why;" I just had to remember it and stay focused on it. For immigrants, the "why" is often tied to their family. When one member of a family makes it out of a developing country to the developed world, it's naturally assumed that they'll support their family back home. This is the immigrant struggle; it becomes the underlying reason you must work harder than others, why you can't take a break, and why you go the extra mile. Someone back home is depending on you.

Often, your family members back home don't have the same opportunities you do. They expect you to succeed so that one day you can help them. If you come from a less fortunate family, no matter whether you're an immigrant or not, the expectation is the same: the successful member of the family who succeeded in life helps their family. During one summer trip to Ukraine, I was reminded of my "why" and why it was something I couldn't run from.

It was the summer before my final year of college. I had worked tirelessly for three years, paying school out of pocket and fully supporting myself. I was ready to take a vacation before starting summer courses—a break free from work and school for a few weeks. My hometown, Odesa, is the jewel of the black sea. It's a breathtaking port city with heavy architectural influence from Italian and French styles. With its stunning beaches and amazing social scene, I knew I'd accomplish two things at once: visit my family and swim in the warm waters of the Black Sea, soaking up all the sun I could get.

The wheels screeched as the plane hit the tarmac and everyone clapped as the flight attendant said, "Welcome to Odesa." I was back home, in the land of my ancestors, with a Viking history that spoke to a legacy of greatness among Ukrainians. I felt so much emotion, tears welled in my eyes. It's true that we were a developing country, but what lives in Ukraine is a strong, deep history of resilience, and I knew resilience lived in me as well. It was a strength I had identified early on.

As we deplaned, I met my father at the airport. Seeing him was always difficult because he hadn't been the most active part of my life, and the distance didn't make it any easier. He took me to my grandparents' house, where I'd be staying for the next few weeks. The smells of my grandma's cooking filled the house, and nostalgia washed over me.

As I sat down with my grandparents, I realized my grandfather had a catheter. He explained that he desperately needed surgery. Social healthcare was supposed to cover costs; however, socialism never delivered on its promises. I was devastated to discover he'd already developed a severe infection from the catheter and that the situation was dire. The surgery would cost a few thousand dollars, but they didn't have the money to pay for it. Reality quickly interfered with my summer vacation. I realized I needed to step up and that I had an obligation.

It hit me like a ton of bricks. My family was my "why." If they couldn't have a better life, what was it all for? What was I working toward if not to help them? In that moment, I felt a stronger drive and motivation to succeed than ever before. I had to do it for them because they deserved to spend their retirement years in comfort and peace. Somehow, I'd get them to the United States. I used all the money I had to cover the surgery. I didn't have any savings because I'd used every penny to stay out of debt while going to college.

We scheduled my grandpa's surgery in a private hospital, and before I knew it, surgery day arrived. As they wheeled him away, he smiled, grateful beyond words. While he was in surgery, I took my grandma out for lunch to keep her mind occupied, as she seemed stressed about the procedure. After I got her talking, she opened up about how hard they'd worked their entire lives and how challenging it was living under communism. She shared how they'd lost everything in the fall of communism, when their savings turned into worthless paper that couldn't even buy a loaf of bread.

I realized the enormity of what they'd lost in life and what they'd endured when freedom of speech or religion wasn't possible. That day in the restaurant, I realized I didn't just owe it to my grandparents to succeed, but also to the many generations that had come before me. Grandma shared with me how, in the 1800s, my grandpa's family had been forcefully removed from their land in Ukraine and sent to Bessarabia, now modern-day Moldova. Ukrainians have been fighting for their freedom and independence throughout the history of the region, facing conquests from the Mongols to the Ottomans.

Queen Olga was the regent ruler of Kievan Rus, the first East Slavic state that covered modern-day Ukraine. She was a military leader and a legend who defended Kyiv, the current Ukrainian capital. With support from the army and her people, Queen Olga changed the system of tribute gathering in the first legal reform recorded in Eastern Europe. That day, from deep within me, arose the drive to succeed—my "why." I owed it to myself, my mother, my grandmother, her mother, and even Queen Olga, who drowned her enemies in the Dnipro River. Their sacrifices had to mean something.

Returning to the United States a few weeks later, I vowed to be the greatest success my bloodline had ever seen. I worked differently because I was driven on a cellular level that no one could fully understand. When you find your "why," the energy it brings will propel you forward with such intensity that you must learn how to steer yourself effectively. Take the time to dig deep to discover your own "why." Go back and ask yourself the questions I posed earlier. Your "why" is the most important factor in a success mentality. Until you have it, you can't go anywhere in life.

When you figure out your "why," test it out with your grand vision, which should be broad—you should be thinking about the big picture.

II. THE BIG PICTURE

If I had to bet money on it today, I would wager that you don't have a clear vision of the life you want. In fact, you probably don't even have a vision for the next five to ten years. This must change—today. How can you get anything out of life if you have no idea what you want? Without a clear vision, you risk aimlessly wandering through life, merely getting by. It's not a purposeful or intentional existence, and you need to work on this.

Your mind, and every cell in your body, functions like a computer. It needs to be properly programmed. When you think of the big picture for your life, you start an incredible programming sequence in your mind. I don't mean thinking about what's going to happen tomorrow, but where you see yourself five to ten years from now. You don't realize it, but by simply allowing your mind to believe in this vision, you pave the way for it to be possible.

This is a critical barrier to overcome. Your mind begins to see and process all things and situations without limit. Instead of saying, "I can't afford that trip," your mind naturally starts thinking of ways to make the trip affordable and creating a plan to get there. It's what I call limitless thinking.

Be a limitless thinker by removing the barriers you may not even realize exist. Reprogramming your mind opens up a world of possibilities. You don't need to know how to get there. First, think about the big picture and remove the limits from that vision.

The big picture is your far-off vision. Stop thinking small. Do not sit there and tell me, "I want a nicer car." That's pathetic and small thinking. Envision a garage full of nice cars and houses in multiple countries—that's thinking big. When we think small, we limit what's in store for us. The universe has warehouses full of blessings waiting for you, and you're sitting there envisioning a storage shed.

The challenge of thinking big is that you're not really sure if you deserve more. Something deep inside always triggers self-doubt. Kill that voice and remind yourself daily that you deserve more. If you don't kill the voice, it'll never let you dream big. Now, picture the dream in detail.

Start with a list. Don't be shy. No one is reading your mind, so think hard about what you want to see in your life. Here are some ideas to get you started:

- Millions of dollars?
- A huge house?
- Nice cars?
- Good spouse?
- Early retirement?
- Supporting your family?
- A college degree?
- Getting in the best shape of your life?

- Luxurious vacations all over the world?
- Running a business empire?
- Being your own boss?
- A large family?

Whatever you envision, there's a 99 percent chance you have no idea how to get there. That's normal, so have no fear. Creating your vision was only the first step. Whatever it was you envisioned, glue that image in your mind.

From the big picture, start breaking down the next ten years, and the next five years. I find it much easier to operate in five-year increments. Think of the top ten things you need to achieve in the next five years to support your bigger vision. These things will become crucial as we work on your plan. At this stage of the process, don't worry about how you'll get there. Keep the big picture central in your mind by writing it down and keeping a running list of what you'd like to do in the next five years.

In my big picture vision, I envisioned becoming a millionaire, living a life of travel and luxury, and enjoying an international career. I imagined blazing a trail in a male-dominated world, immigrating my extended family to the United States for a better life, owning a big home, having a supportive partner, and enjoying limitless financial success in all aspects. I broke these goals down into ten-year and five-year segments. In my five-year segment, I realized

I needed to form a company to avoid relying on anyone else. I made it my mission to figure this out.

Eventually, I did it. It was just me for a while. I was in my early twenties, trying to make it out there in the big world. My consultancy grew over time, and I couldn't have imagined that one day another firm would approach me to do international work all around the world. I went from working on smaller projects to large-scale projects, and from working between just a few states to traveling across five continents. I visited over eighty countries.

By having a big-picture vision, I gave my mind the freedom to plan for something that initially seemed unattainable. Every small step I took in those next five years moved me slowly toward my goals. Finally, unexpectedly, those steps led me to be in the right place at the right time.

Within the first year of opening my mind to opportunities, the floodgates opened, unleashing a surge of possibilities. The positive momentum continued, even though I had no idea how I'd get there at the outset.

III. NOT KNOWING HOW YOU'LL GET THERE

Knowing how to execute your vision may seem somewhat impossible. When you begin so far away from your destination, the distance you perceive it will take to get there may feel unattainable. I assure you that it's not as impossible as it seems. I came from the streets of a post-communist country—with no English, no money, and no connections—and achieved my goals, which is proof that you can, too. You're most likely starting off in a much better position than I did. Accept the fact that you don't need to know exactly how to get there. The path will gradually open to you, and you'll start moving with intention because your mind has been programmed like a computer. You'll naturally gravitate toward things that lead you to what you envisioned. You'll intuitively know what works for you and what doesn't. The only thing you can't lose sight of is your vision and your "why." Keep those programmed in the back of your mind. Think without limits; be limitless.

Like you, I had no idea how to execute the wonderful fantasy I had dreamed up. I didn't know what *would* get me there, but I knew what *wouldn't* get me there. Once I accepted that an entry-level job wasn't suitable for my experience, I returned to my city and started networking. When I embraced the fact that I deserved better, more opportunities came my way.

After the political dust settled, I got offers for smaller consulting work in the political arena. I knew I needed a company, yet I had no clue how to create one. Not knowing how to do something is not a reason to avoid doing it.

Buck up and learn. I called a friend of mine, Daniel, who was a lawyer, and asked him to register a company for me. To my surprise, it was inexpensive.

Imagine my surprise when I showed up at the bank to open a business account, and the banker asked me for the business tax ID number. I was like a deer in the headlights. I didn't have a number, and I had no clue how to get one.

In that scenario, many people would have let fear take over, but I was over being afraid of what anyone thought. I reminded myself to be confident and smiled at the banker and said, "I'm sorry, I don't have one. Maybe you could guide me on how to get one quickly. I'm new to this and would appreciate your help." A massive grin lit up her face; one I will never forget. A weight came off my shoulders as she guided me to a computer, pulled up the United States tax site, and showed me the simple process of getting a tax ID number.

Within five minutes, I had a tax ID number, and in fifteen minutes, I had a business bank account. I'll never forget that story, because when I walked into that bank, I knew I was going to be a millionaire, even if I had no clue how I would get there. All I knew was that I was taking steps in the right direction.

I believed strongly that I was destined for more, and that belief pushed me to strive for more. I wasn't afraid to admit what I didn't know, and I didn't let embarrassment or shame wash over me. Instead, I swallowed my pride and accepted that I didn't know much, but could learn. I learned to ask for help and that there's no shame in that. In fact, there's more shame in not asking for help.

More importantly, I realized that you don't need to know how to turn your vision into a reality. The funny thing about this story is that I ended up cofounding a law firm with my friend Daniel. I didn't know then how I would accomplish any of it, but in the end, I accomplished even more than I set out to do. Do not be intimidated by your own potential; it exists for a reason. That being said, it's also important to be somewhat realistic when things don't go exactly as you envisioned. Sometimes your vision needs a little bit of adjusting.

IV. BEING REALISTIC WITH YOURSELF

Not being realistic with yourself from the start of your journey can create a great deal of failure and disappointment later. I'm a big dreamer, but even I must admit that dreams require a dose of reality. You can be a limitless thinker while also being realistic. Start by creating realistic expectations of yourself. There must be a sense of reality between your vision and your strengths and talents, and they should be somewhat aligned. If you're built like a football player, you cannot decide the next day that you're going to become a world-famous ballerina. This is an unrealistic expectation.

If you pursue a career that brings you closer to your vision but continually hit a wall, you need to realize you're in the wrong field. When your strengths don't match the career path, it's perfectly acceptable to be realistic and switch careers. The sooner you have that reality check, the faster you can get on the right track.

You can only fail so many times before realizing the shoe simply doesn't fit and that it's time to recalibrate. Adjustments are part of the process. The adjustments I made saved me a great deal of headaches later in life. Even though no one really supported my decision, I knew what was best for me and was realistic about my strengths and which paths weren't suitable.

There's a long line of doctors on my father's side. Oddly enough, he isn't a doctor. From the day I was born, there was an expectation that I would also grow up to be a doctor. Remember that other people's dreams and visions are not your own. I never wanted to be a doctor, but my family's influence was so strong that, as I entered high school, I questioned whether I wanted to go to medical school. In fact, when I graduated from high school, my mother was already telling everyone I was going to be a doctor. The pressure was on. This is where I needed a dose of reality.

First, this wasn't my dream, and second, I was never strong in subjects like biology, chemistry, or math. I couldn't even stand the sight of blood, and every time I had my blood taken, I fainted. If it had truly been my dream to become a doctor, I could have gotten over my fears, but it wasn't.

The reality is, when you try to accomplish someone else's vision for you, you rarely succeed because motivation and drive will be lacking. Remember, this dream is for you. You may have a purpose behind it, such as supporting your family, but in the end, it's for YOU!

I enrolled in college as a pre-med major; which is the degree meant for medical school preparation. Never in the 18 years of my life did I apply myself like I did then. I had no friends and I studied every weekend, but in the end my grades were average. I couldn't imagine what I could do to improve my academic performance. Despite giving it my all, I would never make an all-star doctor at that rate, and I hated every second of it. In fact, with average grades, I wasn't sure which medical school I could get into.

When you're on a path that isn't true to your vision, you'll feel the misery and find it hard to stay motivated. This is a clear sign the path isn't for you. This isn't to say you won't have bad days when you're working toward your dream vision, but you'll instantly know the difference. It just won't feel right—you'll be giving it your all and still end up with average results. My average grades meant my talents and skill set simply didn't match, and I wasn't feeling motivated. Everything felt forced. The universe was blocking my path, and the results reflected that.

The day came when I'd had enough. My organic chemistry professor was handing out our graded tests. I received a low B, which wasn't the end of the world, but it felt like the end of my world that day. I had studied for weeks for that test, convinced I was one hundred percent ready. The dose of reality I needed hit me that day. No matter how hard I tried, I was simply hitting the average marker on that career path. Why in God's name would I work that hard, have no life and no friends, just to be some version of average and live out someone else's dream? It was a sign.

When you start recognizing the signs, you become much wiser. I have never felt more motivated and in control of my life than I did when I walked out of that class. That day, I accepted that I was never going to be a doctor, and that was great news. I could stop pretending I'd be the next doctor in the family and finally just be Vlada.

A rush hit me as I walked out of that class. I ran to the administrative building, right to the main office, and swung open the door as victorious and loud as ever, and said, "I'm Vlada Galan, and I'm changing my major today." The office fell silent, and they all stared at me. I'm sure they had no idea why I was so loud and authoritative.

One friendly administrator handed me paperwork, while the other tried to make cheerful conversation. "What are you changing your major to?" she asked.

"I have no idea," I said, "but pre-medical isn't for me." They seemed even more puzzled. As I perused the long list of majors, I was dumbfounded. I had no clue what to choose. Economics didn't require taking chemistry classes, so I picked that and submitted my paperwork.

To this day, I still feel the excitement and adrenaline of that afternoon. I'd taken charge of my destiny, and knew with absolute certainty I would succeed in a different career path.

It's amazing what happens when we take the bull by the horns and face the hard reality that something or someone just isn't meant for us. It was as if heaven's doors had opened. I felt motivated like never before and started reading books on economics and politics, and it all came so easily to me. I had a social life and a job, and I earned A's without even trying hard. Every morning, I was excited for classes and my professors regularly commented on my participation and contributions.

Let me be clear: changing my major didn't suddenly make me an overnight success, but it cleared the path for something that was meant for me—something I could be passionate about. That all started with a small dose of reality and being realistic.

Are you being realistic about your goals right now? Whatever path you're on, are you just going with the flow, or are you taking charge and leading the life you want? Chances are you're not taking charge, but I'll bet you've taken the first step by acknowledging that there's more to learn out there.

Years from now, when you look back, you'll realize those small epiphanies were life's biggest game changers. It's through small actions that we end up changing course and working toward some of the biggest successes.

CHAPTER TWO LESSONS

1. Understanding Your "Why"
- Your "why" is the sense of purpose that drives you. Without it, pursuing goals can feel meaningless.
- To discover your "why," reflect on what brings you fulfillment, your core values, and what you're passionate about. This intersection defines your purpose.

2. Self-Reflection Questions to Help Uncover Your "Why":
- Are you happy with your current life?
- Do you think you deserve more?
- Who is most important to you?
- Who do you want to see you succeed?
- What do you want to prove in your life?

Answering these questions can help identify your motivations and aspirations.

3. Visualizing the Big Picture
- Many people lack a clear vision of their future. Start thinking about where you see yourself in five to ten years.

- Allow your mind to envision great possibilities without limits. This mindset shift opens up new opportunities.

4. Creating Your Vision
- Write down your dreams and what you want to achieve, which might include financial success, personal fulfillment, or helping your family.
- Focus on the big picture first and don't worry about the details of how to achieve it at this stage.

5. The Journey to Your Vision
- You may not know how to execute your vision at first, but being open to learning and adjusting is crucial.
- Take actionable steps toward your vision. The more you focus on your goals, the more opportunities will arise.

6. Being Realistic
- While dreaming big is important, it's essential to align your aspirations with your actual strengths and abilities.
- Adjust your vision if necessary, especially if your current path doesn't resonate with you or produce satisfaction.

7. Making Informed Decisions
- Reflection is key to ensure you follow your own dreams and not those imposed by others.
- If you're feeling discontent on your current path, consider making changes to align with your true passions and interests.

Discovering your "why" and creating a vision is a transformative journey. It's important to dream big, reflect on your passions, and stay realistic about your capabilities. By taking charge of your purpose and aspirations, you can initiate meaningful changes that lead to a fulfilling life. Embrace the process of uncovering your true self and take the steps necessary to achieve your dreams.

CHAPTER TWO EXERCISE

The Big Picture and Finding Your "Why"

If you could achieve anything you wanted in life, what would it be?

What do you envision in your "dream" life?

Is it making millions of dollars? Owning a house? Retiring early? Getting a college degree? Running a business empire?

From this big picture, break down the next five years of your life.

What are the top ten things you need to do in the next five years to help you reach that bigger vision?

"What is your why?

I'm going to deliver your "why" on a silver platter. All you have to do is fill in the blanks.

Don't overthink your answers.

WHY?

1. because you deserve more,
2. because _____ is counting on you,

3. because you need to prove to _____ that you can do it,
4. because you were made for more
5. because you deserve to be happy because of _____.

Once you figure out your "why," test it out with a broad, grand vision.

CHAPTER 3

BELIEVE YOU ARE WORTHY

Knowing what you want means absolutely nothing if you don't believe you can have it—or worse, that you're unworthy of such great things. Whether you're the most confident human being on the planet or the least confident, we all face self-doubt.

There's one key ingredient in the recipe for success, and that's believing you're worthy of it. Not believing in your worth has serious negative consequences. I cannot save those who cannot save themselves. So, get serious about this and listen carefully. Stop the self-sabotage. You read that right. Doubting that you're worthy of good things in life is nothing short of self-sabotage. The enemy is not outside; it's within you. You're fighting against yourself and detracting from your own success by harboring low self-worth and not believing that you can have all the incredible things life has to offer.

When you maintain a limited mindset, you miss every opportunity for growth and success. Your thoughts hold immense power over your life. What you think about daily, you attract. It sounds like a gimmick, but it isn't.

Think about it: If you believe you deserve an incredible life, you'll begin to see opportunities at every corner. Your senses become heightened, allowing you to perceive the world around you as full of opportunity rather than stagnant and depressing. Conversely, when you don't believe you're deserving, you'll see only negatives that reinforce your mindset.

Stop limiting your potential. Your only competition is your potential. Start believing you can have it all and deserve it all. Live every day with the mindset that life is a gift and that you're capitalizing on it. Treat each new day as a new opportunity for a small win. Win at your work meeting, win at the gym, and win by getting that extra discount on your insurance. Just win. Spend each day getting something extra out of it for yourself. Forget everyone else. Screw the system designed to make you believe you're a slave to your circumstances, your employer, and your taxes for the rest of your life.

Live for yourself and win for yourself every day. If someone is rude to you, put them in their place so hard that they never come back for a second helping of the kick-ass you just dished out.

Be in it for you. Elevate from the trenches, get on the playing field, believe you deserve to be there, and play to win. Every time you look at a successful or confident person, remind yourself that they've been in low places, and it's their belief that got them to the other side. That belief is what determines part of the outcome—your belief that YOU can do it and that YOU are worthy. You don't need to know the "how" right away. That will come with time. Just believe.

On one particular occasion, I believed in myself, and it paid off in spades. It was a warm August day in Salzburg, Austria. The light mountain air was as intoxicating as the beautiful landscapes around me. I was working on a political campaign for the Chancellor of Austria. It was a big deal, and I was only in my mid-twenties. I was a college graduate, and by that point, I had built a nice political career in the United States. Finally, I was working internationally, and it was a dream come true.

As I sat in a huge room full of men at the party headquarters, I suddenly felt small. Did I belong here? Was I worthy? I went through my exercise of the Three A's (Affirm, Accept, and Act) to keep the feeling of imposter syndrome at bay. When I reached the action part, I realized I was ready for some big moves. I wanted a higher-level university degree to feel more accomplished. To me, it was essential. I thought it would give me more confidence as I continued in this robust international career.

The more I sat there and took notes on the meeting, the more I realized I needed to go big or go home. During that meeting, I googled Harvard master's degree programs. Ivy League seemed unrealistic, and I didn't exactly feel worthy, but I was determined to address that nonsense thinking. If all those men in that room could sit there feeling high and mighty while looking down on a young woman in their field, then I could absolutely believe in myself enough to crack the Ivy League code. I had the strengths and skill set to do it.

I told myself I would one day walk into the room as an Ivy League grad and be more educated and articulate than all of them combined. The sequence was initiated; I programmed my computer, and no one would stop me. That deep-seated belief, triggered by the spark of motivation, ignited the flame. The lesson I learned in Salzberg was that if I believed I could do it, nothing would stop me, even if I didn't know how I would accomplish such a big goal. Eventually, I found the path because I trusted the process. I took the first step, and you should, too.

I. YOU ARE ENOUGH

The next challenge in the sequence comes in believing you are enough. Was I enough for Ivy League? What does it mean to believe you are enough? It doesn't mean what you think it means. I'm not referring to whether you're smart and educated enough or have the family backing and money to be deemed enough. What I mean is: Are you mentally tough enough? If you are, you can climb mountains you never knew you could climb. It means you're tough enough. Your current circumstances mean absolutely nothing compared to your mental toughness. Life is going to get ugly at some point. It's going to throw you the kind of curveballs that make you want to crawl under a rock and disappear for a while. Trust me, the game of life isn't for the faint of heart. Building up your mental toughness is critical to survival and success.

You may be thinking to yourself, "I'm not tough." Perhaps you aren't today, but that doesn't mean you can't be. Having a hard life doesn't make you tough if your coping mechanism is going out and drinking all weekend to "release" your stress. That shows you're quite weak and haven't enabled yourself to level up; instead, you choose the escape route. Mental toughness is showing up every day. It's built by consistency without vices or unhealthy coping mechanisms. It's the grueling day-to-day schedule that requires showing up that builds character and mental toughness. This teaches you that you must face your reality to change it.

Where are you in life right now? Are you in a miserable job with no vision for where it's going? Are you struggling to accept the reality of your financial affairs or spending frivolously on useless, unnecessary things? Are you in a bad relationship with no apparent way out? Are you just getting by?

The way to believe in yourself is to stand up for yourself first and foremost, and that helps build mental toughness. Just like I stuck it to everyone in my family by not becoming the next doctor, you can stick it to yourself and everyone else by changing something now.

Think about the current circumstances in your life. Do a vulnerability assessment on yourself: what areas do you have little control over and hate profusely? Practice makes perfect, so choose something easy to change. Over time, you'll build the skills to face the harder issues on your list. For example, if your issue is going out every weekend, start by limiting those outings to only two weekends a month, and then scale that back to one weekend a month. Fill the other weekends with a consistent activity that replaces your "escape" activity—something that matches your big vision. If your dream is to be a lawyer, start filling your weekends with taking practice tests for your law entrance exam. Alternatively, go to a gym activity or start a weekend self-care routine to better yourself. If you're a social butterfly, look for a local community adult sports team to join for fun.

The activity you fill your weekends with should be something that makes you better. At first, you won't love the changes. The old, weak version of you will want the comfort zone, but comfort zones don't make us tough or successful. You'll miss the "escape" activities you're used to; however, through the process of showing up to better yourself, you'll develop a discipline and mental toughness to face challenges instead of fleeing from them. This is a key building block of the success formula. Start building a life that you don't need to escape from.

After coming up with the grand plan in Austria to pursue a master's degree from an Ivy League university, the hard work began. Instead of watching mindless movies on my long transatlantic flights to see clients, I changed my habits and instead prepared my applications and studied for entrance exams on the flights. Working full-time made it essential to find time in a schedule that didn't allow for much flexibility. I stopped going to the useless happy-hour socials and swapped them out for writing application essays.

I had to get disciplined, and I hated it. It was all too easy to say, "I have a good job and a decent salary, and I deserve to relax now." I had to toughen up to get more out of life. A second degree was what I wanted and needed to demand my seat at the table, gain the experience to get to the next stage of success, and build my own table.

To get there, I had work to do. I had to assess myself and figure out what I needed to change to get the job done. I started to work out consistently, eat better, and take my vitamins. While my friends focused on cocktail hours and buying new Chanel handbags, I was saving every penny to pay for an Ivy League university and spending my nights studying.

I applied to Harvard and was accepted. You'd think I was overjoyed and excited to tell everyone, but quite the opposite was true. I was so scared I wouldn't be good enough or able to finish my degree, I kept my acceptance a secret. I started with a part-time schedule and flew to campus, keeping the biggest secret in the world. Even while finishing my degree, I continued working. That took immense discipline, but I only grew stronger from it.

The interesting part of this whole story is that when I was sitting in Austria, coming up with the bright idea of going to an Ivy League university, I had no clue how I would get there, but I believed I would. Day by day, the path opened in front of me, and I grew tougher by working harder. I stepped out of my comfort zone, never having imagined that a year later I'd be flying to Boston for orientation, much less graduating two years later from an Ivy League master's program.

What you're going to learn is that, the moment life feels even slightly comfortable, it's time to shake things up and get moving. When things become comfortable, you've hit a plateau. To reach the next level, you must be strong enough for the journey. So, toughen up, because you're not going anywhere if you stay in your comfort zone.

11. YOU ARE ONLY AS STRONG AS YOUR SUPPORT SYSTEM

When you begin working on yourself and believing that you harness a greater power than you ever knew was possible, extraordinary things start to happen. As you ascend to new heights, you'll realize that your ability to reach these heights is directly tied to the kind of support system you have around you. Your support system will determine your success or failure in life. This is one of the greatest lessons I can teach you.

What you'll learn is that most people around you are dead weight; the bigger your circle, the worse off you are. We'll delve into this a little later. So, how do you identify your support system?

Among the group of people who may consider themselves your friends and family, only a small select few are "die-hards." Those are the people who 1) are never envious of you and always seem genuinely happy for you; 2) always check in on you, even when you don't stay in touch; and 3) never ask for anything.

It's crucial to understand who you're surrounded by. The die-hards are those who gain nothing from supporting you and don't operate on any sort of agenda. They never ask for anything and always take the time to make sure you're okay. Most importantly, they believe in you, even when you don't believe in yourself.

These people are difficult to find, but we all have them. You just need to look around your circle and identify them. For me, it was always my mom and my childhood friend, whom I've known since second grade. Over time, I added a few more members to my support system, including a few girlfriends from opposite sides of the world who I knew would be my rescue crew if I ever needed one.

Your rescue crew may not be the people you spend time with regularly. Often, they don't appear on your lunch dates or nights out. Even though they're not necessarily the group you hang out with, they're still the real deal. Rarely will you find your support team on shopping dates and lunches, they're the behind-the-scenes crew. They're not there for the show; they're there for you—at your worst and best. You can count on them to listen, bounce ideas off of, and, most importantly, give you a reality check when you need it. They're often the only people who will tell you the truth rather than only what you want to hear. They aren't the "yes team" that'll support your stupid ideas and make you feel like a genius. Sometimes, they're the "no team," which can help you gain perspective and recalibrate. They're the most valuable assets you'll have in life.

Can you identify a few people in your circle whom you consider your support system? If you can't, it's not the end of the world. You'll find them along the way. A support system doesn't necessarily consist of people you've known for ages; these people can appear in various chapters of your life.

I was working on a presidential election in the Balkans in the early years of my career. It was a challenging environment for a young woman. My candidate was the former president of the United Nations General Assembly, yet he didn't take a female consultant very seriously. His team was horrible to work with and lacked vision in every way. I felt frustrated every day in this hellish rollercoaster of a campaign.

The silver lining came when I met Jelena, a young Serbian woman, who made every effort to connect with me, and we quickly bonded. Jelena also had a horrible experience on the campaign, but I realized she was different from others I'd met along the way because she had no agenda. She didn't want anything from me and asked nothing of me. Jelena always went above and beyond to check in on me during the campaign, and I realized she really cared and was a genuine human being. She had a heart of gold, and I valued our friendship. I never got the impression she was jealous of me. Together, we became pals, and through that campaign, she became my one-person support system. Unfortunately, the campaign continued to spiral into disaster, and we had to drop the client. Jelena left shortly thereafter as well.

After I left the country, we stayed in touch periodically. Eventually, she moved to Dubai, and we reconnected there on one of my trips. We picked up right where we left off. Eventually, I bought a second residence in Dubai and saw her more frequently. What amazed me was that, without a shadow of a doubt, I could always count on her to listen and support me. No matter how successful she or I became, we never envied each other. I supported Jelena when she needed me, and I knew she would do the same for me.

Jelena was someone I hadn't initially identified as part of my support system, but I found her along the way, and she was the real deal. She came to me for career advice, and I went to her for relationship advice. She never steered me wrong, and her support was invaluable. We built a beautiful friendship—one that I cherish to this day.

Don't be discouraged if you haven't yet identified someone who can be part of your invisible support system. Just like I found Jelena along the way, you'll find your people along the way. Trust the process and learn how to identify them. Don't let them slip by.

People who believe in you at all costs are your people—your support system. They'll support your belief in having it all and be there cheering you on when you get there.

III. THE SPARK OF MOTIVATION

Without knowing what motivates you, it's hard to believe you can succeed. It becomes challenging to get that first big push you need to get yourself in gear. Motivation is the engine that will drive you. You don't need motivation every day to get through daily tasks, you will have to rely on discipline for that. However, you'll still need a spark of motivation in the beginning to get started. Even the most disciplined people struggle to execute something that was never ignited by motivation.

Finding your motivation begins with examining what it is you're passionate about or what frustrates you enough to take action. Passion aligns directly with motivation because it's usually what excites us. This passion can serve as a real motivation force for you to succeed. If passion isn't what ignites you, then find your purpose. It's based on your core values, and often you'll see that your purpose is something much bigger than you. Part of believing you can have it all is having the drive to pursue the bigger vision.

Anger and frustration can trigger another motivation for that drive. Both can be huge agents for change in your life. Like it or not, anger and frustration push us into gear and ignite a flame that, if channeled the right way, encourages us to act. These feelings often force us to find solutions to deal with changing our predicament. Finding that spark will either come from your passion, your purpose, or your anger and frustration, and often, it comes unexpectedly.

I was three years into my college degree, majoring in economics, when I realized I'd amassed the same amount of political science classes as I had economics. I took them as electives, but enjoyed those courses so much that I couldn't stop. There I was, about to graduate, but uncertain about my major. Not sure what to do, I consulted with my college advisor about whether I should make political science my major.

As I walked into her office, she took one glance at me, visibly annoyed by my presence, as if she didn't take me seriously. While I may have looked like a peppy dumb blonde, I was far from it. Blonde wasn't even my real hair color. She sized me up based on my looks—something I would get used to in life and use to my advantage as being underestimated. I explained that I really enjoyed political science, and that I felt it was a career path I could pursue.

She laughed gleefully. "Really," she began, "is it because economics classes are just too hard for you?"

I felt a bit flushed. Did this woman think I was dumb? "No, Mrs. Alice," I replied, "If you looked at my grades, you'd see I excel in economics just as much as political science." She sat up a bit, as if I had her attention.

"Well then, why on earth would you pursue a career in a field you'll never be able to get a job in?"

Was she serious? The degrading manner of the conversation ignited a flame that still burns today. I was infuriated. I looked her dead in the eye. "Alice, I'm changing my major to political science. Economics will be my minor, and I don't think you know me. I will always have a job in my field."

She seemed stunned that I dared to respond so firmly. She backtracked swiftly, explaining that it was easier to find work with an economics degree. I accepted her attempts to smooth over the awkward situation, but it was clear she understood that sitting across from her was someone much smarter than she had given me credit for. Her assumption that I couldn't succeed made me so angry that it sparked my motivation.

I was already passionate about all things politics, but someone telling me I wouldn't succeed became the fuel in my engine. I began volunteering on political campaigns on weekends and reading books on political survey research and the data science behind elections. I was determined to learn about this field of work inside and out. No one had to push me to do these things. I was self-disciplined enough to pursue them. I wanted to succeed in this career so much I could taste it. I got my first job in politics the year I graduated. It's funny to think it was all thanks to my advisor, who claimed I'd have no career in politics.

Years later, the university invited me to speak to a group of students. Funny enough, my advisor was in the audience. She came up to me afterwards and congratulated me, saying she'd always believed in me. This time it was I who laughed, and I thanked her politely.

There have been many "Alices" in my life who claimed I couldn't do something, or wouldn't succeed. I've used their doubts and criticisms to go far in life. Take every naysayer in your life—every single person who's said you would fail—and use their doubts to your advantage. Your passion, fueled by their doubt, will become the motivation you need to believe in yourself and go the distance.

CHAPTER THREE LESSONS

1. Believing in Your Worth
- Knowing what you want is meaningless if you don't believe you deserve it.
- Self-doubt leads to self-sabotage, making you your own worst enemy.

2. Power of Thoughts
- Your mindset can either open doors to opportunities or trap you in negativity.
- When you believe you deserve great things, you start noticing chances for growth.

3. Potential and Competition
- Your only competition is your own potential; belief in your abilities is key to unlocking success.
- Live each day with a positive outlook and seek small wins.

4. Mental Toughness
- Being mentally tough allows you to overcome challenges regardless of the circumstances.
- Life will throw adversities at you; resilience is essential for survival and success.

5. Taking Action
- Assess your current situation and identify what you can change.
- Start with manageable steps to build confidence and discipline.

6. Support System
- Your success is influenced by your support system, which should consist of those who genuinely support you without an agenda.
- Identify your "die-hard" supporters who will be there through ups and downs.

7. Motivation
- Motivation is necessary to get started on your path to success. It can stem from passion or frustration.
- Use other people's doubts as fuel for motivation, turning negativity into drive.

Believing in your worth, building mental toughness, and surrounding yourself with a supportive network are essential for pursuing your goals. Motivation, whether from passion, purpose, or overcoming negativity, drives you toward success. Small daily actions are key to building the life you desire.

CHAPTER 4

STOP DREAMING AND START WORKING— THE PLAN

Believing you can have something and that you deserve it is critical to getting to the working phase of taking control of your life. Working on a plan to achieve your big vision is the first real activity that requires you to roll up your sleeves and get dirty. Up to this point, you've been dreaming up the big vision and learning to believe in yourself, but now the proof is in the pudding. Will you actually get to work and make a plan?

Most people don't achieve their life goals because they cannot execute what they're mentally invested in. Not having a plan marks the beginning of the end for your dreams. No one has accomplished anything significant by wandering around aimlessly, hoping success would fall from the sky. Success will never come without a plan and the committed execution of that plan.

Operating without a plan has many dangers. Without a plan, you'll lack direction and have a hard time focusing. It can become incredibly difficult to know what steps to take if you're not operating off a plan. You'll lose focus and waste valuable time. You can easily become sidetracked and miss key opportunities.

Right now, you may feel like you're too busy to formulate a plan, but the reality is you're simply not being productive. Being busy means nothing if you're aimlessly running in circles without a plan, wasting time, resources, and energy. You'll burn out fast, become depressed, and lose motivation. You'll need a plan to reach your pinnacle of success. A plan enables you to work smarter rather than harder. A journey of a thousand miles begins with the first step. Today is the day you take that first step, and that means putting together a plan.

To succeed, you'll need to work off a plan for each and every significant goal in your life. This process will start over and over again with each new level of success. Become a master at setting goals, making a plan, and executing it. You'll go through this process many times on your journey to success.

After spending a decade accomplishing my big vision, I began thinking about the next decade. Years of spending sixty hours a month on a plane, circling the globe, made me aware that I couldn't rely on my energy and health forever. One day I'd get tired and need a cushion to fall back on. I needed a plan to generate passive income so that whenever I felt like taking off for a year, I'd have the freedom to do so. It should never be the money you're after; it's the freedom that comes with having enough money to do whatever you want. That's the real dream.

I began studying real estate and looked at emerging markets all over the world where it was booming. The Middle East seemed to be an amazing case study for real estate success, so I shifted my focus there, and quickly realized the Abu Dhabi and Dubai real estate markets were prime for investment. The returns were astonishing, and the world's wealthiest individuals were pouring their money into the United Arab Emirates.

I wanted to get serious about buying property, but first, I needed residency status to make the process easier. Then, I needed to free up some finances to reach that goal. At the time, my money was tied up in various assets, so I planned to set money aside specifically for property investment. Eventually, I started a company focusing solely on real estate investments.

I followed my plan religiously and eventually purchased my first rental property. Before I knew it, I had friends interested in investing, and my company began managing other investments. By having a plan and sticking to it, I remained focused and capitalized on opportunities. As I crafted each new plan, my vision grew.

Today, I have a strong real estate portfolio that provides the cushion I sought. I never could have imagined it growing into what it is today. Operating off a plan forced me to maintain financial discipline, enabling me to get where I wanted to go.

I. THE GOAL

Everything starts with a goal. At this point in your journey, you should have a grasp of what you want out of life and a big-picture view of it. However, what you don't yet have is the plan. Drawing out a plan sounds daunting, but it isn't. It's much simpler than you've led yourself to believe. A good plan requires a goal and milestones along the way. To make a plan, you need to narrow down your goal. While there will be multiple goals to plan for in life, start by focusing on just one for now.

I'll walk you through the steps of setting a goal, but first we need to work together on understanding what a successful goal is. It needs to be full of **purpose** and align with the big picture you dreamed up for yourself. We discussed your "why" earlier, which summarizes your purpose. For example, to achieve your "why," you may set a goal to become a millionaire. This is a great-big picture goal, but you need to break it down into digestible portions to include in-between goals along the way, typically yearly. If this is the big-picture goal, then you'll need building blocks along the way.

First, you must assess your current situation. If you're stuck in a dead-end job, you'll spend your entire life in that hamster wheel. To switch jobs, you may need more education. In this example, your first milestone may be to complete a new certification or get an additional degree. In that case, your short-run goal is to research schools, apply, and begin classes.

A successful goal is **challenging**; it should push you to grow, but not break you. Instead, it should force you to get to work. A successful goal should also allow room for change and be **flexible**, as you never know what life may throw at you. So, if you become derailed, adjust your goal to be more manageable until you reach the next milestone. A successful goal has these three components: 1) Purposeful, 2) Challenging, and 3) Flexible.

The next step in creating your goal is to define it clearly, set a time frame for accomplishing it, and remain relentless in your tenacity to achieve it.

I'm a firm believer in the SMART framework, which was developed in the 1980s by a corporate planner to set clear, attainable goals. I use this framework from time to time when I'm struggling to set a goal properly or feel I'm not setting the right goal.

SMART stands for:

Specific—Be specific about what you want to achieve.

Measurable—Make your goal measurable. Put benchmarks in place to measure your success.

Attainable—Set a realistic goal. Don't make it too easy, but be careful not to make it so difficult that it becomes unattainable.

Relevant—Set a goal that matters to you and aligns with the bigger vision that fits into your five-year plan.

Time-bound—Establish a time frame to accomplish your goal.

This framework can help you set a goal easily. The faster you do it, the faster you can start drawing out the plan to achieve that goal, so don't put it off. Someone else is already out there doing it, so why aren't you?

I know all about setting goals. Many people have attempted to deter me from accomplishing my goal, but I overcame those challenges, and so will you. Stay strong, resilient, and true to what you set out to do.

During my early career, I had the honor of working on a presidential campaign in Africa for a sitting president who was running for re-election. When I took on the campaign, I knew it would be a significant time commitment, and that there was a good chance the president could lose his re-election. Financially, it was a lucrative project, but losing the election could have negatively affected my career.

Like everyone else, I wanted to work with consultants who had strong win records, especially if I wanted more business in Africa. When I discussed this opportunity with my mom, she put it to me very clearly—"What is your goal?"

It was to expand my consulting footprint to the African continent, as I had already worked in Europe and North America. For me, Africa was uncharted territory. When I explained my goal, she told me I had only one option: accept the campaign, but under the condition that I focus solely on that for the next four months. She knew there was no other way to achieve victory without laser focus, which meant living, breathing, and immersing myself in the campaign. She told me victory should be my only target because it would serve as a milestone toward my bigger goal. Without a victory, there would be no other strong projects to pursue in Africa.

Soon afterward, I packed my bags and set foot on the African continent. Everything was different—the food, the people, even the work process. It was a huge learning curve. I dug deep to the core of my being and remembered my goal every morning.

It wasn't long before my campaign caught the eye of the American Embassy, which was closely monitoring the election. I was surprised to be invited to the Ambassador's Residence. I was young and naive enough to think it was just a pleasant meeting to get to know each other, but quickly realized they didn't love having me around. Perhaps they preferred the other candidate. The Ambassador didn't say it directly, rather gently leaned over his chair, and said, "Vlada, would you like to meet the other candidate? I'd be happy to introduce you." Was he serious?

I saw it for what it was. How could I jump ship in the middle of the election? That could jeopardize my goal of victory. To be quite honest, the approach intimidated me. I was so focused and successful in the campaign that I had his attention. Well, he should have paid attention to me then, because I was mad.

When you're on the brink of accomplishing your goal, someone or something will come along to deter you. I'm not sure why life tests us this way, but it feels like a final obstacle we must face before reaching the finish line. This serves as a test of our commitment to our goal. I realized that despite being young and a bit nervous, I had a goal, and I harnessed the power deep within myself to reach the finish line.

That meeting reaffirmed that I was getting close to the prize. I took another sip of my whiskey on the rocks and said, "Ambassador, we both know that isn't a good idea. Thank you for the offer, but I must kindly decline. I thought the United States doesn't engage in regime change." His face grew pale; I had put him on notice.

The rest of the election felt like a blur as I worked tirelessly. Election day came, and I had been in the country for four months, focused on nothing else. Everything was riding on that day. That night, we won the election by less than a percentage point. I had done it. It was challenging, but it meant something to me. There was a bigger picture in my mind—I'd unlocked the African continent. The potential was unparalleled. I was in. I had done it. Shortly thereafter, the United States Ambassador left.

II. THE PLAN

Accomplishing a goal doesn't happen by accident; you need a plan. If you don't know where to start, you're not alone—this feeling is normal. Begin with a working plan, which should be laid out in six-month to twelve-month increments. If that feels overwhelming, start with three months. Take out your calendar and get to work.

First, start with your day-to-day commitments. Pencil in weekly workouts. This is non-negotiable; you need energy to get places, and without a weekly workout plan, you're going to be sluggish, foggy-minded, and undisciplined. Aim for a minimum of three workouts each week. Start with that and build from there. Don't tell me you can't or don't have the time. If you have time to scroll through your social media, make pointless phone calls, and watch TV, you have time for the gym. These are aimless activities that accomplish nothing. You can spare three to four hours a week for yourself—put the workout plan in place and execute it.

If you're like me and get bored easily, switch it up and do different workout activities during the week; it doesn't have to be stale and boring. Feeling better leads to increased productivity and looking better, and no one has ever complained about that. The next part of your plan needs to include one growth activity per month, which means either scheduling a networking event or setting aside time to work on a new skill that brings you closer to your goal.

Set milestones in between your current position and your end goal. Initially, this will all feel unnatural or uncomfortable, but don't get discouraged. Our minds need time to be rewired. They say it takes 21 days to create a habit, but in my experience, it takes closer to ninety days for a habit to become a permanent lifestyle change. This is the 21/90 rule. To make new habits stick, you need to rewire your thought process for it to stop feeling foreign. Keep in mind, we are not striving for perfection here, but rather movement and actions.

Over the next six months, the plan you set must pave the way to accomplishing your goal. If your objective is to change jobs in the next year, your monthly plans should include networking events, mentorship, and improving your skill set. Every week, engage in at least one activity that strengthens your position to achieve your end goal. Aim for a variety of activities that fit into this category each month.

I wanted to keep working in the political sphere, which meant I had to get serious and continue building my network. I'd gotten lazy, and while I had a plan in place, I wasn't working off that plan. After a serious reckoning with myself, I realized I had to roll up my sleeves and take actionable steps. The first thing I did was pencil in a monthly event hosted by the local political party I was affiliated with. They organized a monthly breakfast at a local country club, where the surrounding counties held their respective monthly political meetings. The county I belonged to had the most high-end political breakfasts with the highest attendance in our city. The event also drew a crowd from surrounding counties.

Every third Saturday of the month, I dressed to the nines and made my appearance. Truthfully, at first, I hated it. I didn't know many people there, so I had to force myself to approach new people and strike up a conversation. I knew, deep down, that these were simply excuses. Who wouldn't rather sleep in on a Saturday morning than have to work? I killed those excuses and attended the monthly breakfasts, often against my will.

As a result, my contacts in the political sphere of my state grew immensely. Those organizations were all connected and had statewide chapters. What started out as a dreaded monthly obligation turned into an opportunity to get to know everyone in my field. Whenever I needed a favor, there was one degree of separation between me and any political contact. That was in 2012, and I still rely on the contacts I made back then. In fact, most of those individuals have become governors, senators, and members of congress.

In fact, I recently boarded a flight and saw one of those breakfast contacts who'd served as a Senator, and then became an Ambassador to one of the most critical countries for the United States. His phone number was still the same, and we had a great catch-up conversation. The investment I made more than a decade ago continues to serve me today.

III. THE COMMITMENT

Commitment is a fundamental part of any success formula. How committed are you to your future and the big dream you envisioned? The answer better be "very committed" because there's no other path to success. Simply put, a lack of commitment is a lack of discipline.

Lacking commitment is a problem we all face. Something more exciting than an existing obligation comes up, or we become lazy and quit following through. This issue can destroy progress. If you want to waste your life away, this is the way to do it. At first, it seems so innocent—you blow off one meeting, don't finish an important task, miss an important work event, or skip an important class.

What you're training yourself to do in these instances is allow for an exit plan from the original plan you designed. These occurrences will become more frequent, you'll get used to letting others down at work, at home, and worst of all, you'll become accustomed to letting yourself down. This is literally the highway to hell. The more you quit tasks, the more comfortable it becomes. Stop living in your comfort zone. Get used to being uncomfortable.

Commitment means being persistent and disciplined, even when you don't feel like it. It requires focus. If you don't feel like attending that extra networking event, tough luck. Suck it up and get out there. I hate to admit that, 90 percent of the time, I didn't feel like doing half of what I've done. However, that didn't stop me because I was committed.

It's important to remind yourself of the goal you set and the purpose behind it. Every time you don't feel like doing something on your plan, remind yourself why you're doing it, and say no to anything and everything that doesn't align with your goal. The main difference between successful people and those who aren't is that they do the work, no matter how they feel. You're not always going to be motivated, so don't count on motivation—rely on your commitment.

Pushing through is one of the most important things you can do. The more you push through tasks you don't want to do, the easier it gets. If you've ever been skiing, the first few days can be insanely challenging; however, as you navigate some small slopes, you gradually build confidence. This process gets easier and easier with each ski run, and before you know it, you're getting into the groove.

I'll never forget when I faced a moment where my commitment was truly tested, and pushing through wasn't as easy as mastering skiing. The COVID-19 pandemic was a tough one for all of us. Travel was restricted, countries were shutting down, and it felt as though the world was ending. I had taken the last flight out of Ukraine in mid-March before the airport closed down in Kyiv. Upon landing in the USA, I realized I didn't know what would happen to my business, clients, and the entire multimillion-dollar consultancy firm I'd built. My clients included foreign governments, heads of state, high net-worth individuals, presidential candidates, political parties, and foreign companies.

I began to fear the worst: I'd lose my clients and the business I had built. With the world in lockdown, I couldn't do my job, travel, or coordinate lobbying meetings in foreign capitals. No one would hold elections during such uncertain times. During the first two months at home, I stayed active and committed to my plan. I continued working as much as I could, but I became increasingly more worried as clients lowered their retainer, or stopped paying, or attempted to cancel contracts altogether.

By May, I realized I had to figure this out. I had become a millionaire by the age of thirty, and it finally felt like I had broken through in life. Then came 2020, and I felt I could lose it all. I hadn't had a chance to properly invest money or even enjoy this incredible new life status. My goal for 2020 had been to double the income I'd earned. I knew it was ambitious, but you should know by now that I don't aim low. How could I stick to the plan? How could I achieve my goal now? "Push through," I told myself.

One morning, while having coffee with my mom, I expressed my concerns about work. She wisely said, "People make money in wars and natural disasters, so why can't you make money during a pandemic?" She had a point. I could either suffer through it, or find a way to solve problems during the crisis and capitalize on them. I realized I was restricting myself, so why wasn't I thinking outside the box?

The next day, I started calling clients and asking what their governments needed to address COVID-related challenges. Many expressed a need for supplies, while others sought public relations plans related to COVID safety measures. I recognized that I had a significant opportunity and started calling everyone I knew in the medical field. Within a week, I sold masks to one of my clients. Suddenly, I was selling supplies where I could, all while managing crisis work and helping clients navigate the public relations side of the crisis.

In fact, I became so in demand when I repositioned myself and pushed through that I had to book flights to see clients just two months after travel restrictions were implemented. I had no other option; multiple presidential offices wrote letters on my behalf for immigration. No one was flying to any of the places I was visiting, and many airlines had stopped servicing some of those destinations altogether. Occasionally, my clients had to arrange private jet travel for me to reach them.

What began as the biggest obstacle and deterrent that year became my biggest success. I faced the fear of losing it all, but it was my commitment, grit, and drive to push through that forced me to recalibrate. Despite the challenges, I exceeded my goal. Even a global pandemic wasn't an excuse to bail on my goal or fail to execute my plan. In fact, it was one of my best working years. I flew on more private jets than I could count, made more money than I ever thought possible, and proved to my clients that I wouldn't back down. I've held many contracts with clients since then thanks to the trust I built during that time.

It was no accident that everything turned out so perfectly. I had the right mentality—the success mentality. I didn't sit at home depressed, overeating, or drinking my heart out. Instead, I remained committed and pushed through. While facing the unknown again was scary, I emerged on the other side of it, accomplished my goal, stuck to the plan, and achieved an overwhelming success. I wouldn't have it any other way, and neither should you.

Your commitments will be tested, so remain dedicated, stay the course, and trust the process. You can spend three years working with slow, steady progress, and then in the fourth year become the biggest success with multi-millionaire status. You'll find that you're the most fulfilled you've ever been in your life, but it won't be possible without commitment.

CHAPTER FOUR LESSONS

1. The Need for a Plan
- Many people fail to achieve their goals because they lack a plan for executing their ideas.
- Wandering without a clear direction hinders focus and productivity, leading to wasted time and missed opportunities.
- A plan helps you work smarter and reach success without burning out.

2. Setting and Implementing Goals
- Achieving success requires setting a structured plan for each significant goal and revisiting this process as new challenges arise.

3. Components of a Successful Goal
- Goals should be purposeful, challenging, and flexible.
- Goals must align with your overall vision and include measurable milestones to track progress.
- The SMART framework can guide effective goal setting: Specific, Measurable, Attainable, Relevant, And Time-bound.

4. Creating a Working Plan

- Start your working plan by breaking it down into manageable timeframes, focusing on immediate commitments.
- Incorporate regular activities that contribute to achieving your ultimate goal. For example, set aside time for networking or professional development each month.
- Establish consistency in your routine, as it takes time to build new habits.

5. Commitment to Your Goals

- Commitment is essential for success; it requires discipline and persistence to perform tasks when motivation is lacking.
- Reflect on your purpose and remain focused on your goals to combat distractions and challenges.

To achieve long-term success, commitment to your plans and goals is essential. Staying dedicated through challenges can lead to fulfilling milestones, making the hard work worthwhile. Embrace the journey with the mindset that your dedication will ultimately lead to significant accomplishments.

CHAPTER 5

DROPPING DEAD WEIGHT

There is a famous phrase: "Tell me who your friends are, and I'll tell you who you are." Like it or not, we are defined by the people around us. The company we keep determines our success. Sometimes, we don't understand why we aren't getting anywhere in life. You may feel confused or be searching for explanations for the current stagnation in your life. The reality is that if you analyze those around you, you'll often find dead weight.

Having people around you who leech off your time, finances, and energy will get you nowhere, no matter how great your plan is, or how disciplined you are in accomplishing it. Being around people who drag you down affects your mental, emotional, and even physical well-being. Often, you cannot see how negative these people are because they surround you so frequently that they become the norm. These people can influence your mindset negatively, often appearing pessimistic. They're best described as energy vampires. Their constant complaining and negative sentiments impact how you see the world. If their daily habits don't match yours, and they always pull you away from being disciplined, they become obstacles to your success.

You cannot pursue a success mentality with people like that next to you. They'll stunt your growth, and you'll naturally begin to doubt yourself and your abilities in their presence. Surrounding yourself with people who don't uplift or inspire you can significantly affect your happiness. The only way to reach a successful place in life is to cut them off. Like a cancer, they must be cut out of your life, leaving no traces behind. Never allow them to find their way back to you. You'll need to undergo a transformative process of assessing everyone in your life who has regular access to you. During this time, lean on your support system, as we discussed earlier.

Get serious and set boundaries that protect your peace of mind. Do not let anyone cross those boundaries, and when they do, cut their toxicity out of your life. Cutting someone off means limiting contact. Do not reach out to them, do not attend events they invite you to, and do not fall prey to their small-minded manipulations. Stand firm in your decision and do not cave. Forgiving doesn't mean forgetting and making the same mistake, or letting them get close to you again. Don't be shy about being straightforward. If they keep harassing you, even after you've put physical and emotional distance between you, tell them that the relationship isn't serving you anymore and that you have chosen to focus on yourself. There is no other way.

When I finished college, I left my job working at a bar to transition into a career path. For me, the bar was just a college job, nothing more. It paid well for the hours I could work, and it helped me accomplish my goal of finishing college debt-free. I always had a goal in mind, and I didn't fall prey to losing my focus. Many other college students also worked at the bar, and most of them lost sight of why they were there in the first place. Instead, they dropped out of college, falling into the lifestyle of the entertainment industry filled with parties, alcohol, drugs, and meaningless relationships, which wasn't for me. I stuck to my plan; however, that didn't mean I didn't occasionally go out with them for dinner or drinks. Periodically, we'd get together and go out. For me, it was harmless fun that had its limits. For them, it became a lifestyle since they had nothing else going on.

When I graduated and left my bar job, many of the people I knew still tried to get together with me. When we saw each other, I noticed a pattern: they consistently questioned why I needed to be in such a serious career. They instilled self-doubt as they pointed out that my entry-level salary was much lower than what I used to make working with them, and that I had no freedom anymore. This one-track thinking wasn't for me, and I realized I'd outgrown them. I was going places they weren't. The answer was simple: I needed to cut them off.

There was value in the career I wanted to pursue. I knew where I was going, but they weren't going to the same place. I isolated myself completely. It wasn't easy; I was too busy working to make friends in college, so the only people I was around were people from work. I was firm in my decision to cut them off, and I stuck to it. By opening the space in life, I made friends at my new political job. We got together for networking, happy hours, and steak dinners.

The shift was immediate, and I could feel the growth and progress in my new surroundings. These new colleagues were going places. They were educated, well-read, and analytical. It was a different world. Instead of having drinks until three in the morning, they attended networking events and fundraisers. They spent their weekends discussing new political and business strategies over lunch, weekday mornings at the gym, and evenings planning for the next day.

A common purpose united us. We were all involved in politics because we wanted to bring about positive change. I'm still friends with many people I met during my first political job. Our careers and relationships have developed over the years. None of this could have been possible if I hadn't dropped the dead weight.

I. SHRINKING YOUR CIRCLE

Dropping dead weight isn't easy. In fact, it can be one of the hardest things to do because we form attachments to people, memories, and our idea of what these people represent in our lives. Sometimes, people fill a gap, but we don't let them go after the fact because we've formed an attachment.

Having a large circle can be a significant energy drain, and if you're draining your energy, you're not operating in what I like to call "optimal mode." This elevated mode of your inner being allows you to move quickly and intentionally to get results. Getting to optimal mode isn't easy, and it requires sacrifice. I didn't fully realize how much sacrifice it took until I experienced it firsthand.

You must understand which friendships serve you and which ones don't. With practice and time, this will become one of your essential life skills. Do you currently have a large circle of friends? Do you know how to identify who is a real friend and who isn't? Like me, you probably learned these lessons the hard way.

Here are the lessons I discovered: 1) not everyone is your friend, 2) you cannot have time for everyone, 3) you don't need more friends than you can count on one hand. To grow, you'll need to shrink your circle of what you call "friends." Shrinking the circle starts with understanding which of the three categories people fall into: 1) your inner circle, 2) acquaintances, or 3) professional and extended network.

Having clear categories helps you classify the people in your life faster. By placing them into the right categories, you can properly manage your time with them and protect yourself from potential problems down the road. Let's break down each category.

Inner Circle

Your inner circle is the most sacred group of people in your life, and it must be protected at all costs. It comprises a few trusted family members and a select few friends. The friends in the inner circle must be the most honest, loyal, and trustworthy people you know. There are no exceptions to this rule. Your inner circle should be comprised of no more than five people.

You can have family members who are not your best friends; there's nothing wrong with keeping them out of your inner circle. Having a large inner circle exposes you to risk. The inner circle of friends must be the people you can tell your deepest, darkest secrets to. Likewise, the inner circle family members must be the first people you want to call when something is wrong.

If you have a large friend group and are a very social individual, you must realize that not all these people can be classified as part of your inner circle. Energetically, you don't have time for this, and you'll see for yourself that not everyone is in it for you. You'll end up feeling betrayed by these people because, to them, you're not part of their inner circle. Just because they call you a friend means nothing, so don't be fooled.

Real friends come through not with words, but real actions. Inner circle friends would go to the ends of the earth for you. They're in it not for themselves but for you. These friends are hard to find, but once you find them, they stay around for a long time, if not a lifetime. This doesn't mean they cannot exit your life, because they can. Not everyone can climb as high as you will climb, so remember this.

Acquaintances

Most people around you should fall into this category. An acquaintance, by definition, is someone you know but isn't a close friend. If you have a large friend group, you'll need to move eighty percent of that friend group into the acquaintances category. These categories are only for your own classification. There's no need to announce to people that they're no longer your closest pals.

Be smart about whom you spend time with, share information with, and whom you count on. Experience has taught me that most people around us are dead weight and present more problems than they're worth. This is why it's necessary to clean up your circle. Acquaintances should never be the first to know anything; rather, they should be the last to know. You don't need to give anyone the blueprint for your new life vision or the map of how you'll get there.

Acquaintances may still be people you see for lunch periodically, go out with in your friend group, or even go on trips with. They serve as additional people for having fun and socializing; however, they're not the people whose life problems you should get involved with. If an acquaintance is having issues in her relationship or marriage, that isn't your problem. Trying to take on their problems only puts weight on you. You're dropping the dead weight, not adding to it.

Bringing in acquaintances too closely drains you because you'll get sucked into their issues. They will consume your precious time, and in return, they don't contribute anything substantial to help you climb higher. Stay friendly, polite, and social, and let them serve a purpose in your life, but never fall into the trap of believing they're your inner-circle friends.

Professional

The professional part of your circle is the key to growing your net worth. Since you're someone who wants to go places in life, this is the golden category of relationships you should focus on. This is why it's so important to clean up your inner circle. By moving people into the right category, you can take the time to focus on a whole different area of your life. It doesn't matter what career path you want to take in life; you need contacts. This is by far where most of my focus goes when it comes to how I spend my time. I have made my professional network a priority. Your connections are where the money is made. I dedicate a tremendous amount of time to keeping my professional relationships warm. I check in with my professional contacts regularly, rather than allowing them to go stagnant, and I'm always working an angle on what I need from them or offering to help them. Helping your professional circle is not an energy drain; it's an investment. You rack up professional favors that you can cash in on when you need something.

I cannot overstate the value and importance of your professional circle. These people are not dead weight; they are golden. However, as wonderful as this network can be, there's always someone who will try to abuse your time. If someone like this emerges in your professional network, distance yourself from them. They'll get the point. Keep it balanced.

I wish I could say that my college experience was easy or super fun. The reality is I was working 60 hours a week while going to school full time. It was exhausting. I wasn't born with a silver spoon in my mouth; instead, I was born into a communist country and had no college fund or trust fund to fall back on. I didn't have many friends in college because my schedule didn't always allow for socializing. This was intentional; I understood the value of my time and that my energy was limited.

There was one friend at work with whom I got along quite well. Diana was originally from my part of the world, and the immigrant bond connected us. She was pretty and intelligent, but very shallow. I quickly realized that she only cared about money, dating rich guys, and material things. Some of her values clearly differed from mine. I also sensed a demeaning nature in her. She always seemed to attempt to prove she was better at everything, which created a strange undercurrent of jealousy that manifested in strange ways. I cared about her as a friend from the bottom of my heart; however, as I transitioned from my college job to working in politics, she became increasingly jealous. It was a strange situation. At times, I felt she was happy for me as I started this new chapter of my life. She even brought me an incredible gift to celebrate my first job in politics, but there was still an undercurrent of jealousy.

I came to realize it's not that people wish you ill; instead, they feel sorry for themselves. They often lack self-confidence, which leads to jealousy or self-pity. The truth was, Diana was going to a better university than I was, and she would soon graduate and enter an amazing career field. So why the jealousy? Perhaps it stemmed from her frustration at not yet being in the next chapter of her life? I really didn't understand it. I always considered her a close, inner-circle friend because her actions seemed to show that she was supportive of me.

We often traveled together, and she started dating a wealthy guy. Ironically, she convinced him to move into the building I was living in. It always felt like a competition. Of course, her cash-rich new boyfriend got a nice penthouse, much nicer than my one-bedroom flat. He showered her with lavish gifts, and I was genuinely happy for her. However, all she came to care about were expensive handbags and shoes, and that was all she talked about.

When Diana's birthday came, I scraped together enough money to get her a present and plan a birthday trip to Miami. The gift was a $600 tote from a mid-level designer brand, which was a lot for me to spend at the time. I bought the gift with my whole heart. On her birthday, I couldn't have been more excited to give her the present and watch her expression as she opened the box. It saddened me that she looked unamused by the gift. It was evident that it didn't match whatever standards she had set for an acceptable designer gift.

As we sat at her birthday dinner days later with a few close girlfriends, I leaned over and said, "I hope you liked your gift."

Diana laughed and replied, "Well, it's Tory Burch, not exactly a Celine bag like the one Adam got me." It was a defining moment as she sipped her martini and I realized the naivety of that friendship from my side. There I was, fully invested in the friendship and completely supportive of her as a person. I had given her a gift from my heart because I always wanted the best for anyone I considered a friend. Yet, on the other side of the table sat a shallow, empty individual who didn't reflect my values. I realized she wasn't a real friend. Diana valued the intention behind a gift that a man twice her age—with ten times more resources than I had—had given her, rather than appreciating that I scraped together whatever remaining funds I had to buy her something nice. It was nothing for him to buy her a $3,000 handbag, but it had taken everything for me to buy her a $600 one, and she knew that.

That moment has never left me. I was elevating into the next chapter of my life with an incredible career and realized it was better not to have any friends than to have fake friends like Diana. Such friendships would only deplete me mentally and emotionally. That day, a switch flipped, and I suddenly recognized that Diana was dead weight. She would never be a real friend or be truly supportive of me, so I had to cut her out. She was using me as a friend of convenience.

Knowing what I know now, I would have never allowed her into my life, but hindsight is 20/20. Diana came into my life to teach me the valuable lesson of dropping the dead weight. This lesson has served me well.

Are you ready to clean house? Are you prepared to eliminate everything that isn't serving you? I will warn you that it isn't easy, and losing a friend wasn't easy for me. However, after the incident with Diana, I just stopped contacting her. I told her she had hurt me deeply, and no matter how many times she apologized, I had no desire to work it out. I didn't even keep her as an acquaintance; instead, I cut her out completely. When someone shows you their true colors for the first time, believe them. Don't wait for round two or three of that behavior.

I forgave Diana, cut her out of my life, and moved on. What's interesting is that when you step up to protect your energy, you withdraw it from the people feeding off it. It was interesting to watch Diana drop out of a top college and end up at a lower-level college. She and her boyfriend broke up, and she struggled financially. When I took my power back, she lost some of hers.

Being surrounded by the wrong people is a distraction and a drain on your energy reserves. Over time, Diana's life eventually leveled out, but I never had the desire to reconnect with her. She has shown me her true self, and I didn't need to see much else.

11. READING THE SIGNS

Not knowing how to read the signs when someone is affecting your progress keeps you around the wrong circle of people. You cannot allow this to happen. Reflecting on the situation I had with Diana, the problem was that I didn't know how to read the signs initially. They were there, but I missed them because I had no idea what I was looking for. You don't need to make the same mistake.

The first individual you need to remove from your life is the one who holds you back and discourages you from pursuing your goals. Small-minded people hold you back because they consider your goals and ambitions laughable or unattainable. They don't know how to get there themselves, so they tell you it's ridiculous or impossible. The only thing that is ridiculous is you leaving them in your circle. If this reflects your entire circle, then it's time for a new one.

The next sign to look for in your circle is anyone who consistently avoids taking responsibility. They blame others and avoid being held accountable. People who can't take responsibility for their actions will bring you down.

Next, assess how you feel, energetically, around the people in your circle whom you consider friends or acquaintances. Do you feel drained after being around them? If you find yourself naturally pulling away from someone—whether they're a friend, family member, or professional contact—that's a strong sign that you need to distance yourself from them. You are growing, but not everyone is growing with you or at the same pace. They're not going to the same place as you, and the more you try to hold on to them while your instincts reject the idea of doing certain things or spending time with them, the more you do yourself a disservice. Don't fight the feeling; accept it. They're draining you, and on a subconscious level, you feel it.

If you have people around you who always seem depressed or exhibit negativity, this will eventually bleed over into your own outlook. Not only will they never accept your success, they will also criticize your efforts at every turn. They are dead weight.

If you have relationships that feel unbalanced, where you're always the one reaching out or giving up your time and resources to help them, while receiving very little in return, that is a huge red flag. Drop the dead weight and cut them off slowly. You'll see that they either become enraged at your refusal to be used, or they'll disappear completely when they realize you have nothing left to give them. These people are users and can be some of the most dangerous individuals to have in your circle.

Another sign to be aware of is someone who lies consistently. When you catch someone in a lie, make a mental note of it. It didn't happen by accident, it likely indicates a pattern of behavior. This proves that they're not trustworthy enough to stay in your circle. They've shown you a character flaw. Don't let it slip by—believe them when they show you their true colors. If they lie *to* you, they'll also lie *about* you, so steer clear.

Lastly, remove anyone who shows signs of toxic behavior, engages in manipulation, or poses ultimatums. These individuals often create drama from nothing and attempt to fear-monger you into doing things that rarely suit your interests. Their presence will have a profoundly negative impact on your overall well-being. Sometimes it's hard to recognize what's happening in a toxic relationship because it starts out feeling normal. However, the drama begins to fade when you hang around with smarter people. Often, you're up against a narcissist who shifts your reality and gaslights you, making it difficult to see clearly. If someone is causing you stress and anxiety, this is a clear sign that the relationship is toxic.

Last year, I got involved in a business that my friend Sarah had started. I came on board as a consultant to help her expand her business and onboard new investors. I also made a personal investment into the business because I wanted to be as supportive as possible as my friend took on a new, exciting venture.

During the process, we onboarded another investor who seemed charismatic, dedicated, and business oriented. It was someone she had met in passing. The new investor soon positioned herself in Sarah's inner circle, spending excessive amounts of time with her each day, bringing her gifts, and becoming overly involved in the business. It became clear that she was seeking control.

Sarah began alienating her main business partner because the new investor dominated all of her time and attention. She began pushing Sarah into serious decisions about opening new locations despite having no experience or expertise, purely for her own benefit. She dragged everyone through highs and lows, always creating drama whenever she was required to take accountability for her actions.

Within months, Sarah was barely communicating with her business partner and lashing out. The dynamics became more challenging to navigate as the investor began convincing Sarah that she deserved a larger share of the business without additional investment.

From the start, I could see what was happening. What shocked me was how quickly everything played out. Sarah was trapped on the inside and couldn't understand how dangerous and toxic the dynamic was. The business suffered, and Sarah's relationship with her business partner deteriorated. The investor pushed for rash and rushed decisions, and incited Sarah to act against anyone who voiced reason, including me. I tried to shed light on the situation, but Sarah couldn't grasp the reality of what was happening. The investor should have been cut off a long time ago, or confined to her contractual role, which was minimal, but Sarah had let her infiltrate her circle so deeply that she couldn't do it.

As the situation spiraled, I limited my interactions with Sarah and the investor. Each day seemed to bring new drama. The situation reached a critical point where Sarah finally realized how the investor was affecting the business, the staff, and her relationship with her business partner. She gradually pulled back and limited her time with the investor.

When toxic people lose their control and power over you, they tend to spiral. The investor threatened to sue the very company she was invested in. She stopped talking to me, convinced that I was responsible for Sarah's withdrawal.

The signs were there all along; Sarah just didn't know how to read them. It's always easier to see the signs from the sidelines—we all saw them from the sidelines. It's hard to see what's happening when you're caught in the whirlwind. That's why it's crucial to know what signs to look for.

When Sarah and everyone in the business, including myself, drew a line in the sand and began limiting engagement with the investor to business necessities, everyone communicated with ease and worked productively again. If this situation had continued unchecked, it could have spiraled downward, jeopardizing the entire business Sarah had been building.

It's important to recognize the red flags and learn to read the signs of those who impede your success. Usually, the signs are right in front of you, but you may not be accustomed to looking for them. In retrospect, things that didn't seem so obvious become glaringly clear. As they say, hindsight is 20/20. Don't let it get that far. Drop the dead weight before it begins to suffocate you.

III. LET GO

When you grow into the success mentality, it's often hard to let go of people in your life. Some individuals don't want to evolve. Instead, they serve as a reminder of what it looks like if you don't evolve. You can't take everyone along, so these are the people you need to leave behind. They're dead weight.

People who aren't in tune with themselves will deter you from becoming who you're meant to be. Holding onto these people will rob you of purpose, vision, and momentum, leaving you stagnant for life. They can't operate at the higher level you're aiming for. They have served their purpose in your life, so it's time to let them go. Drop the dead weight.

This process of release doesn't necessarily happen when you pull away; sometimes people naturally exit your life. Don't view this as a tragedy; it's a blessing. While it may be painful, it's necessary.

I had an experience that left me puzzled, shocked, and deeply hurt. However, when it happened, I said thank you, because it meant I was moving to the next level. It signaled that I was elevating in every aspect of life. The shift was shocking, but it didn't happen by accident. It was just time to let go. I don't keep many close friends. My inner circle consists of fewer than five people, and while I have many acquaintances who consider themselves my friends, they are merely acquaintances. I've never let them close enough to get to know much about me. This approach has always been strategic. I recognized early on that superficial relationships would drain me, and I didn't have the energy or capacity for them, especially the one-sided ones, so I kept them at an arm's length. I value deep, meaningful friendships. Life doesn't afford us many of those.

I had an inner-circle friend for over nine years. She knew some of the most private things about me. We were related, with her being the wife of my dad's third cousin. She was in a volatile marriage and desired to change her predicament. I told her that if she learned English and proved herself, I'd hire her to help her get back on her feet so she could provide for herself and her children.

Within a year, she learned English and proved she was eager for the opportunity. Over the next eight years, I brought her into my professional world, involving her in my political projects, giving her access to my political contacts, and bringing her with me on 5-star all-expenses-paid vacations. When she fled from the war in Ukraine as a refugee, I provided a large lump sum of money for her to live off. She was my most trusted friend. I trusted her with money, my contacts, and my clients. I even hired her to help run my nonprofit organization in Ukraine during the war.

I never sensed she was overly jealous of me; I thought she was a friend who wished me well. Over the course of ten months, I noticed changes in her. She became incredibly irresponsible, reckless with money, and ungrateful. She completely disregarded her job and abandoned all the basic responsibilities for which she received a salary almost four times higher than the national average. Naturally, I stopped wanting to be around her as much, and stopped taking trips with her.

She told me about other commission-based projects she was working on for someone else, and I was truly shocked that she could say this to my face while receiving a salary from me. It was clear why she wasn't accomplishing anything at work: she was completely checked out. From a professional standpoint, I was shocked, and personally, I was hurt by the fact that she didn't care or appreciate anything I had done. She was working deals on my time and with the salary I was paying her.

This pushed me to close up even further. I should have immediately fired her and shut the door; however, when this happens in your inner circle, it's not so simple. I truly didn't want to accept what was happening. So many amazing things were happening in my life—the expansion of my investment portfolio, incredible work projects, and the preparation to release my book—that I didn't want to accept the reality that she was dead weight. For eight years, I had been her sole employer. She never even sought another job. What began as my attempt to help her get on her feet and leave a toxic marriage ended up with her becoming my responsibility.

She never progressed personally or professionally. Personally, she was stuck dating all the wrong men. Professionally, she never tried to do more or be more, even when working with me, nor did she want to finish the secondary college degree she'd started. Looking back, I had enabled her behavior. I should have pulled my support much sooner.

Her exit from my life was sudden and unexpected. I was in Ukraine checking in on a political project I had launched and visiting my nonprofit organization that had been providing humanitarian aid during the war. The trip was a bit rushed, as I had only given her a two-day notice that I was coming. To my shock and dismay, she told me she was leaving for a few days. As my employee, she had never discussed this trip with me, and I hadn't approved it. I was taken aback that she was telling me instead of asking me.

She had done the same thing in the past, but she didn't realize I knew it. I had other staff members who'd recorded her previous absences. I didn't want to create a scandal and chose to preserve the friendship, but it was becoming too much. Her actions demonstrated such a high level of disrespect toward me, personally and professionally. For her to have reached a point where she could blatantly tell me to my face she was leaving, with no thought of asking permission, was simply unacceptable.

The alarms went off in my head. Everything felt wrong, and I sensed there was much more going on. I felt the oncoming transition and played nice about the trip. I asked her to bring me all the money she had left for our political project before she left, but I wasn't home when she dropped it off. When I got home, only one-fourth of it was there. Tens of thousands of dollars were missing.

I messaged her right away, and she told me she misunderstood. She thought I only requested a portion of the funds for the project start, not the entirety. I felt uneasy, which was strange since I had always trusted her.

That evening, the uneasy feeling lingered, so I checked everything. She had been in contact with our partners in the United States regarding new shipments. These partners were crucial to the work we do. The first place I looked yielded some shocking discoveries.

Imagine my surprise when I checked my nonprofit email, which I usually don't stay on top of, and saw that—for months—she hadn't responded to emails from one of our most critical partners who had sent us millions of dollars' worth of aid for two months. I was copied on all these emails. Professionally, this was appalling, to say the least. On a personal level, I was shocked, and it immediately became clear that there could be no friendship at a place where there was so much disrespect toward me personally. She knew what this nonprofit organization meant to me and that I had often provided personal funding to keep the work going when donations slowed down.

I messaged her about it right away and sent her copies of the email she didn't respond to. It was shocking and surprising when she claimed that she never received the emails. Of course, this was an absolute lie, as I could see she had. I asked her for the password to her email so I could verify her claim. She didn't respond, nor did she call me. In fact, we would never speak over the phone again.

The next morning, I woke up with a deep urge to seek the truth. This inkling is something you should never disregard. When your instincts tell you to look deeper into something, do it. Investigate and get to the bottom of what your gut is telling you. Intuition is a powerful mechanism, and our instincts rarely guide us astray.

I was the administrator on her work email and could easily change her password from my administrator panel. When I reached her inbox, I discovered that the only deleted emails were the ones I had shared with her. She was clearly trying to hide the evidence. She must have been in a rush because there were other unopened emails from two months earlier.

I reinstated all her emails, so imagine my surprise when all the emails popped up, including the deleted ones. What shocked me about this situation was her intention to deceive me. Those were qualities I hadn't previously seen in her. Perhaps I missed the signs, or maybe the friendship had blinded me.

When I asked her about some unopened emails, she blamed other staff members who hadn't even been copied on them. Her lies continued. She stuck to her story that she had never received the emails. I called her that week, but she never responded. She never told me where she was traveling, but all our friends could see everything she posted on social media.

By Friday of that week, I had no choice but to fire her. She never even called to explain the situation and just completely fell off the grid. Imagine—this is someone I had known for nine years, and employed for eight. She had been my closest friend. Can you imagine your best friend never speaking to you again?

What happened over the following weeks and months continued to shock and bewilder me. She lied to my colleagues who had contacted her about the money. She kept promising to deliver it but never did. The situation only got progressively worse. She began playing games with my nonprofit organization, which was delivering humanitarian aid into a war zone. She was a signatory on the organization's documents, and as new shipments came in during the time I was trying to remove her as a signatory, she held up the humanitarian cargo at the border.

This story is hard to share because the betrayal cuts so deep. Through all of it, I realized what was happening: she was dropping out of my life while I was on my way up. Having someone I considered a friend exit my life in such a way was ultimately a blessing because she was holding me back, and I couldn't see it for what it was—she never wished me well and wasn't truly loyal. I was blinded, and in order to achieve more in life, I had to let go of that fake, negative, ill-wisher. I thanked God for the lesson and moved on.

Letting go is never easy, but it opens so many doors. When someone drops out of your life in such a manner, accept it and let go. They aren't meant to go with you. It's easier said than done, but when you look back years later, you'll understand why.

CHAPTER FIVE LESSONS

1. Impact of Negative Influences
- The company you keep significantly affects your success.
- "Energy vampires"—individuals who drain your energy—can harm your mental, emotional, and physical health.
- It's easy to overlook their negativity when you're constantly surrounded by them.

2. Need for Change
- To achieve success, you may need to cut off toxic relationships.
- Begin by evaluating the people you regularly interact with and set boundaries to protect your peace.

3. Shrinking Your Circle
- Emotional attachments make letting go of friends challenging.
- You must identify which relationships serve you and which ones don't.
- Classify people into three categories: Inner Circle, Acquaintances, and Professional Network.

4. Categories of Relationships

- **Inner Circle:** This should consist of a few trusted individuals (no more than five), including family and friends who genuinely care for you.
- **Acquaintances:** Most people in your life will fall into this category. They're not close friends but are there for socializing, not deep emotional support.
- **Professional Network:** Focus on building relationships that enhance your career. These connections are beneficial and can help you advance.

5. Signs to Remove People from Your Life

- Remove anyone who discourages you from reaching your goals or lacks accountability.
- Avoid people who leave you feeling drained or are always negative.
- Pay attention to unbalanced relationships where you do all the giving.
- Be wary of individuals who consistently lie or exhibit toxic behavior.

6. Letting Go

- It can be tough to let go of people who aren't growing with you.
- These individuals can hinder your progress and keep you stagnant.

- Embrace the process of letting go when necessary, as it leads to new opportunities.

Cutting out toxic relationships is essential for personal growth and success. Assess the people in your life critically, and don't hesitate to remove anyone who detracts from your well-being. Understand that letting go is about reducing negative influences and making space for healthier, supportive relationships that align with your ambitions.

CHAPTER FIVE EXERCISE

Cleaning Up Your Circle

Categorizing relationships helps you classify the people in your life more efficiently. By placing people into the right categories, you can properly manage your time and protect yourself from future problems.

Write out a list of all your friends and then sort them into one of the three categories. Limit your inner circle to 5–8 people.

Acquaintances	Inner Circle	Professional Network

Manage how you interact and spend time with each group according to their classification. This will help you become much more productive.

CHAPTER 6

ELIMINATING DISTRACTIONS

The cold, hard truth is that you can't get to where you're going if you don't eliminate distractions. Even the brightest vision and the strongest belief in yourself can't get you to your destination if you're distracted. Distractions deplete your energy and derail you. They're more dangerous than you perceive them to be. Distractions decrease your productivity, lead to poor decision making, reduce motivation, and leave a trail of unaccomplished goals.

To achieve your end goal, you'll need to operate at full speed, and the reality is that you cannot do this in your current state. You'll need to drop certain habits to begin operating in optimal mode. You've already done the biggest part, which is assessing the dead weight in your life and removing toxic people. Now it's time to remove toxic habits and distractions.

Progress isn't possible without acknowledging the negative influences in your life. Start this process by identifying your habits and distractions. Then, identify your "why" for wanting to change these behaviors. Your "why" helps you stay committed to the process of eliminating distractions and weeding out the bad habits. Pay close attention to what kind of environment forces you to lean into those bad habits. That is the environment you'll need to change to have long-term improvement.

Set a clear target for yourself. For each bad habit, establish a specific goal to get rid of it. Tackle one bad habit at a time rather than all at once. Replacing a bad habit with something more productive often works well.

I used to come home from work every day and turn on the TV, spending four hours every night glued to the screen. I justified this habit by calling it my time to relax and unwind after a stressful day. Sometimes I'd fall asleep in front of the television, binge-watching reality shows. Over four months, I realized I wasn't improving myself in any way. In fact, I had grown lazy in every aspect. I wasn't working out, eating healthy, or feeding my mind with anything beneficial, so I exchanged TV time for going to the gym, cooking, and reading. As I got fitter and smarter, I experienced a mental clarity I hadn't previously known.

On average, it takes two to three months to build a new habit and make it automatic. It may be hard to believe, but you can rewire your brain. Daily repetition is key. It helps when you replace old habits with new ones. This fills the time and makes it easier not to fall back into old patterns.

I. IDENTIFYING DISTRACTIONS

Not being able to identify distractions is harmful to your progress. It causes a lack of focus and can make it feel like you don't have enough time to do everything you need to do, leaving you feeling overwhelmed. In reality, you have the time, but you're wasting it on things that don't align with your goal. Failing to identify your distractions leads to the constant feeling of being overwhelmed. In fact, you may be feeling unproductive and overwhelmed right now. The ugly truth is: it's all your fault. You have no one to blame but yourself. However, your current situation isn't permanent. You can change your predicament by identifying your distractions and eliminating them.

What distractions are you currently facing? What habits do you need to eliminate to become the best version of yourself? Maybe you don't know how to identify them or don't consider them real distractions. Well, I'm here to tell you that they're destroying your progress, and that stops right now. I won't let you do that to yourself anymore.

Social media is the first place to start. It's a toxic abyss where you scroll endlessly through meaningless reels and stories. If you're a procrastinator, social media is where you'll waste the most time, purposefully putting off important tasks. It creates a fake reality, which makes you instantly compare yourself and your life, leaving you feeling inadequate. You'll never feel successful enough, traveled enough, or happy enough compared to the lives you see on social media. Stop trying to keep up and stop searching for validation from random people's comments and likes. Social media often promotes false narratives and distorts your view of the news and the real world. Unless your business is social media based, replace this habit and shift your focus.

Other bad habits to change include those that affect your health. If you're unhealthy, you'll never keep up with the successful movers and shakers. It takes energy to reach their level and even more to stay there. There isn't a lot of oxygen at the top of Mount Everest. The summit is a place where only a select few can survive. Space is limited up there, so if you want a spot, you'd better stop eating garbage, losing muscle mass, drinking daily, and smoking.

Prioritize protein in your diet. This is so important that I have to emphasize it—protein deficiency is linked to lack of motivation and depression. How can you go places if you're unmotivated and depressed? And let's not forget about sleep. This is one of the most important and easy changes you can make. Get eight hours of sleep every night, starting tonight.

Next, stop going out all the time. You're not in a college fraternity, so there's no need to drain your energy going out when you haven't even met some of your basic goals. Get used to it. These are not your people for long-term success. If people in your circle go out regularly, find a different circle to be part of.

Clean up your environment and declutter everything. Your personal space should be a calm, relaxing retreat. Your workspace should also be organized to make it conducive to productivity, not cluttered and miserable. Keep your working environment healthy by not overly engaging with colleagues who waste your time by dumping their issues on you. This is just as toxic as clutter. You can be friendly, but have boundaries. These people are distractions. They have nothing better to do, but you do, so get to it.

If you're a procrastinator like me, you need to be honest with yourself about this issue. Divide tasks into smaller parts and schedule a little time each day to work on them. This can significantly reduce procrastination. Leave nothing for later. Later, you'll lose interest . . . later, life goes by . . . and later, you'll regret not doing something when you had the chance.

While many other distractions and bad habits exist, you'll likely overlook wasting time on things that don't yield results. Sure, you can contemplate the bad habits you need to break because they waste your time—many of which I already listed—but what about the things you work on and put energy into that yield nothing? These are situations we allow people to drag us into, free of charge, only to waste our time and provide no real gain. These are the worst kinds of distractions, and they take money out of our pockets. Time spent working on something that yields us no results is time that could have been spent on something we were paid for. This is a trap I have fallen into many times. Learn to identify these situations and sideline people who drag you into them.

I was working on a project with a company in the Middle East that was very interested in entering the mining sector in Africa. They needed introductions at the cabinet and presidential levels in multiple countries, but they were specifically interested in working with me. The prospect of helping them excited me because I knew the investment would be of significant importance to the country they were most interested in. In order not to waste time, we organized a trip to get introductions started before finalizing a contract. That turned out to be a big mistake that I would come to understand later.

The trip went astonishingly well. I introduced them directly to the president, who expressed interest in their investment in the mineral sector of his country, which had gold, lithium, and many other critical minerals that every nation was in search of. I kept the meeting secret and private, so even the media had no idea these talks were taking place. However, weeks went by, but a contract hadn't been finalized. The terms were an issue, which led to constant back-and-forth between lawyers.

During the process, I made the mistake of continuing to work on the project and following up with multiple trips between the two countries. I even hosted their geologists in my home in Africa for a few months while they collected samples from various mining sites. A few months later, I realized this was one enormous distraction from other projects with actual paying clients. They were taking me for a joyride, using my kindness and connections, and playing games to sign a simple contract.

I let it go on for longer than I should have, mainly because they came from a trusted source, and I didn't believe they wouldn't sign a contract. I had to put my foot down and get serious about finalizing the documents, but when I did, they ghosted me. It had been a royal waste of time, and I had no one to blame but myself. I allowed the situation to become a time-wasting distraction, and I knew better.

Months later, they contacted me again, seeking my help. I clearly stated that they wasted my time the first time, and I wouldn't allow it to happen again. Without a clear signed agreement, I wouldn't do anything—not even so much as make a phone call. My message was clear, and they disappeared again. Fool me once, shame on you, fool me twice, shame on me. I was determined never to let it happen again.

I've shared easily identifiable habits and distractions that drain your time, but none of them compares to this kind of distraction—donating your time to doing favors or working on projects for free is the biggest waste of time, energy, and resources. You're undercutting and undervaluing yourself in a big way. People don't appreciate what is free; they take it for granted. I want you to read this as many times as it takes: STOP GIVING AWAY YOUR TIME FOR FREE. This is the biggest distraction, and it isn't always easy to identify. You convince yourself that you're helping someone or working toward something, but in reality, you're being distracted from things that actually need your attention and for which you should be compensated.

Unfortunately, I have fallen into these traps a few times, trying to help a friend or being too trusting of someone. When you eliminate these distractions, it's amazing how much time and power you regain.

II. CHANGING YOUR HABITS

Do you ever wonder how you form habits or why they're so hard to break? Well, you're not alone. I wondered about it myself when I realized habits were often hard to break. Our minds are wired in an interesting way. In short, we're pleasure seekers. Our minds are always looking for a reward at the end of an action, which releases dopamine, the "feel good" chemical. This is how a habit gets stored in our minds. If your brain registers that you engaged in an action, and it immediately felt good, it flags this and stores it in the part of the brain that operates out of our conscious control. This is a problem because it makes habits difficult to break. Habits live in an area of the brain where we lack conscious control.

The habit circuit works like this:

Stimulus—We first experience a stimulus, which can be a feeling, desire, person, or location that triggers us.

Desire—An immediate desire for something, which could be food, a specific action, a place, or anything else.

Action—You take action to fulfill a desire, motivated by the anticipation of a reward.

Prize—Finally, you receive a pleasurable feeling from the outcome. Your mind categorizes this pleasurable reinforcement, allowing your brain to become increasingly effective at triggering it.

With habits, your mind is wired for quick feel-good effects. As we all know, what feels good in the short run isn't good for us in the long run. Changing your habits requires rewiring your brain. The good news is that, thanks to neuroplasticity, if you start a new habit and practice it continually, you strengthen the new neural connections in your brain. The process begins with conscious decision-making and intentional actions. Start with small steps, focusing on one habit at a time.

To break a bad habit, you must break the habit circuit. You can trick your mind by replacing the habit with a different action. Instead of watching TV every day after work, go for a walk or read. You can switch the TV time for the reward of your new habit. Once you've read for an hour, you can watch some TV.

You can also trick your mind into adding a new habit onto an existing one, known as habit-stacking, and it works. For example, if you drink coffee every morning, use that time to review your to-do list. This will remind you of what you need to work on while curbing procrastination.

Don't make the fatal mistake of falling into the all-or-nothing approach. I used to set aside one hour for my daily workout. If I had less than an hour, I'd skip the workout altogether. It was my all-or-nothing mindset. I eventually changed my perspective; even twenty minutes of daily movement is better than none. I focused more on getting into a habit of moving every day, regardless of time or place, concentrating on the activity itself. This helped me remove the mental barrier I had constructed.

When building a new habit, consistency is key. You cannot reinforce neural pathways otherwise. Remember, you're rewiring your brain.

There has been debate about how much time it takes to form a new habit, but in my experience, it doesn't happen in less than sixty days. For me, it began to feel automated closer to ninety days. The reality is that you'll have setbacks and won't always be able to break a bad habit on your first attempt. However, if you're persistent, you'll get it, and if you're consistent, you'll keep it. Don't get discouraged. Remember your "why" at the very beginning of your journey. It's your motivation to break those bad habits. They will hold you back from your true potential, and you can't afford that. Destroy the old you before it destroys you.

Having lousy money habits is one of the most dangerous bad habits. Living without a budget, being in debt, and engaging in impulse spending is a silent killer. One thing that has always been a source of stress and anxiety is finances. I knew I had to get mine under control.

When I got serious about wanting to succeed in life, I fully analyzed my finances. The good news was that I had no debt; however, I didn't have any savings or a retirement plan either. In my early twenties, it seemed premature to worry about my retirement, but I was wrong. One positive money habit I developed was avoiding debt. I worked throughout college and paid my tuition out of pocket, putting me years ahead of many of my friends financially. The bad news was that I didn't know how to save. I had a bad habit of spending all my money each month and not saving any, and I didn't know how to break it.

I started by creating a budget, outlining all my expenses. This helped me figure out how much money I'd have left at the end of the month. I added a line for savings and factored it into my budget. As soon as I got my paycheck, I immediately moved a portion into savings and established a rule that I couldn't take it out unless it was an emergency. I also went through my monthly expenses and realized I was spending a lot of money on morning coffee runs and eating out. I made a line in my budget for these expenses, allowing for occasional indulgence while remaining disciplined to avoid wasting money.

Living on budget was miserable for the first few months. I didn't feel like I could spend my money how I wanted. It bothered me less as I gradually grew accustomed to the structure. Eventually, I opened a retirement account as well.

After a year, I used some of my savings to reward myself with a nice vacation. Within a few more years, my savings became substantial enough to make investments. When I wanted to start a company, those savings gave me the freedom to take that giant step. Those years of discipline laid the groundwork for the success I enjoy today. While I don't need to live on a budget anymore, I still monitor my expenses, and my spending habits have served me well.

III. STAYING DISCIPLINED AND AVOIDING RELAPSE

Relapsing into an environment full of distractions is a problem, but it shouldn't feel like the end of the world. Failure is part of the journey to success. I once read an interesting study indicating that almost sixty percent of people who try to quit smoking relapse within the first six months. You're not alone in failure. Chances are, others have failed to quit the same bad habit as you. What truly defines you is how you pick yourself up and try again. Don't dwell on the fact that you fell back into old habits or succumbed to distractions. Instead, focus on what you can do differently next time.

Consider these questions:

- What triggers caused you to take up the bad habit again?
- What situations caused you to want to do it?
- How will you better prepare yourself next time to avoid it in the future?

Ironically, it's when you start to see actual results that you're most likely to fall back into old patterns and habits that don't serve you. The real secret of success is training your nervous system to handle higher levels of success without self-sabotaging. Self-discipline is the best way not to relapse and engage is self-sabotaging behaviors.

Self-discipline is the ability to drive yourself to take action and maintain focus, regardless of your emotional or physical state. It manifests when you consciously decide to work toward something beneficial for yourself, even in the face of challenges and distractions.

I once worked for a foreign client on a long-term project. Every year, they sent a delegation to Washington, DC, for high-level meetings. I oversaw the coordination of those important meetings. With six months to plan the visits and make each one a resounding success, I got to work right away. However, within a month, work issues distracted me and I lost my focus. I found myself consumed by social events, travel, and other distractions.

As the months went by, I realized I'd been procrastinating. Very few meetings were set, and I had to provide a report on our progress and a tentative agenda. My team took direction from me, and since I was procrastinating, they were too. I was setting a horrible example and realized I had to get into gear quickly. I cut out the work drama and stopped engaging with colleagues who called me just to vent about their problems. Instead, I dedicated a block of time every day to focus on organizing the meetings and coordinating with my team.

Within a few weeks, we put together a solid agenda. I realized I had made the entire process unnecessarily stressful by procrastinating and getting involved in other people's issues, as well as over-committing to nonessential social gatherings. All those distractions drew my focus away from my priorities. The delegation had a good visit, and I thought I'd learned my lesson, but I couldn't have been more wrong.

The following year, I struggled with the same procrastination issue by failing to accomplish anything when I had months to plan, and only taking action when the deadline to submit the final agenda was looming. I had a terrible habit that needed serious work, so I broke it down into smaller steps and set milestones with deadlines for every single project I worked on. I also scheduled regular calls for all projects to create accountability for weekly progress reports with my team. By breaking down tasks and incorporating self-discipline and accountability, I remained committed throughout all my future projects.

While I cannot say I don't put things off sometimes, I no longer find myself in situations where my procrastination has detrimental effects on my success. I relapsed, but I came through it. I remembered why I had started my journey to success, and I refused to let down everyone who was depending on me simply because I struggled with procrastination.

You will likely relapse into an environment filled with distractions and find it difficult to resist bad habits, but that doesn't mean you can't change for good. Put measures in place that force you to be self-disciplined and accountable. Remind yourself of your purpose on this journey, and you'll see it's much easier to stay on track.

CHAPTER SIX LESSONS

To achieve your goals, it's crucial to eliminate distractions and develop better habits. Distractions can drain your energy, lower productivity, and prevent you from reaching your potential. Recognizing and addressing these distractions is essential.

1. Effect of Distractions
- Distractions hinder progress and lead to unaccomplished goals.
- Recognizing and removing distractions is necessary for maintaining focus and energy.
- Social media and unhealthy habits are common distractions that need to be addressed.

2. Identifying Distractions
- It's important to acknowledge what negatively affects you.
- Identify bad habits and their negative effects on your life.
- Consider how your environment contributes to these habits and make necessary changes.

3. Changing Your Habits
- Replacing bad habits with new, productive ones is crucial.

- Consistent practice is required to build new habits; neuroplasticity allows for rewiring your brain.
- Focus on one habit at a time and avoid the "all or nothing" mindset.

4. Stay Disciplined to Avoid Relapse
- Accept that relapses can happen; it's important to learn from them.
- Identify triggers that cause you to fall back into old habits and create strategies to avoid them.
- Self-discipline is key to maintaining focus despite distractions.

The path to success requires a commitment to eliminating distractions and changing habits. Acknowledging and addressing distractions enables you to stay on course and achieve your goals. Building new habits takes time and persistence, but with discipline, it is possible to maintain progress. Remember to stay focused on your reasons for change and take measures to hold yourself accountable on your journey toward success.

CHAPTER SIX EXERCISE

Identifying Your Distractions

What distractions do you currently have?

What bad habits do you need to break to become the best version of yourself?

Habit Circuit Analysis
Go through the habit circuit and identify the components of each habit you listed: stimulus, desire, action, and prize. Determine how you can break one part of that circuit to break or replace the habit.

Stimulus
The initial trigger that prompts a reaction. This can be:
- A feeling (e.g., stress)
- A desire (e.g., craving for comfort food)
- A person (e.g., a friend who encourages unhealthy habits)
- A location (e.g., a café where you usually indulge)

Desire
The immediate urge or craving that arises after the stimulus. This could be:

- A desire for a specific food (e.g., sweets)
- A wish to engage in a particular action (e.g., scrolling through social media)
- A longing for a place (e.g., going out instead of staying in)

Action

The behavior you take to fulfill the desire. Examples include:

- Eating the food you crave
- Checking your phone or social media
- Going out to socialize instead of working on tasks

Prize

The reward or pleasurable feeling you receive from the action. This can be:

- The comfort of eating (short-term satisfaction)
- The enjoyment of social interaction
- The escape from a task or responsibility

CHAPTER 7

EXECUTION IS KEY

Not executing the plan you've set for yourself means you'll never achieve your goal, much less realize the big picture you envisioned. Having a vision and goals means nothing if you cannot execute them. Execution is the bridge between fantasy and the reality of what exists in your life. I don't want to be the bearer of bad news, but the numbers don't lie: more people fail than succeed when they don't follow through on a plan of action. Just look at the goals people set for New Year's resolutions. Why is it that only nine percent of Americans who make New Year's resolutions actually execute them? It's a daunting statistic.

My point is that only the dedicated survive. Don't become another sad statistic—get serious. You must learn to be disciplined and consistent. It's crucial to identify when you're executing something that isn't part of your plan. Only then can you get back on track. If you don't figure this out, it may seem like you're executing a plan, but is it really the one that will get you where you want to go?

The solution is to evaluate yourself regularly. Ask yourself: Is this taking you to where you need to go? Are you moving closer to your goal? Assess yourself monthly. What did you accomplish in the last month, and do those accomplishments align with your goal? You'll often find that they don't. You'll find yourself living in survivor mode, simply getting by. Life is too short for that. In order to thrive, realign yourself and execute your plan. I had to face this reckoning myself, and the realignment was the scariest step, but I pushed myself to do it anyway.

I've worked for one of the largest public affairs firms in Washington, DC. Although I had previously led my own company, being part of a larger and more powerful firm aligned better with my goal of expanding my strategic capacities. It was a good fit because they didn't dictate who I took as clients or control the type of work I did. My revenue share with the firm in my senior role was also fair and lucrative. From the outside, it looked ideal—I had a prestigious firm behind me, I was doing well financially, and my clients were doing well. It seemed like a perfect fit, but the red flag was that it felt comfortable.

The company split in half when the two founding partners had a falling out, which prompted me to assess myself and my position at the firm. The new shift became uncomfortable and forced me to assess my situation. I quickly realized that, while it was comfortable, it didn't align with my bigger plan of growing multiple businesses outside of my day-to-day work. I was limiting myself to activities that centered only around that job, which didn't leave time for anything extra. My clients were loyal to me, not the firm, so why was I dedicating my day-to-day activities to something that didn't align with my big picture plan?

I expanded my work to include other activities that somewhat aligned with my plan. Yet, I soon realized I needed to return to focusing on my own company and expand my work footprint in other areas outside of that firm. I cannot express how difficult it is to leave a comfortable position with a guaranteed paycheck to go back to having nothing to fall back on but yourself. The more I looked around the firm and saw people who had been there for years, earning barely more than I was, the more I understood that I was off track.

Realignment isn't always fun. I left the firm, and while it was nerve-wracking, it allowed me to start four new companies, continue my consultancy, and even expand it with an office in the Middle East. By assessing myself, I realized I was on a path that wouldn't give me exponential growth. While it felt comfortable for the time being, it wouldn't bring me the twenty-fold growth I desired. Every day I stayed there meant sacrificing my dreams for someone and something else. It was a terrifying change, but looking back, I can see that what I accomplished once I returned to my plan is truly impressive. My self-assessment helped me recognize that I was off track.

Do not be afraid to take a cold, hard look at your life right now. Assess whether you're on the path you want to be on. Are you walking toward one of your goals or just taking the easiest path? There's nothing scary about admitting the truth to yourself. The first step is to admit you have a problem with where you are right now. Without this admission, you cannot realign yourself to get on the path you need to follow.

I. TOO MANY GOALS

Setting too many goals will cause big problems. Having multiple goals within a short timeframe is overwhelming, resulting in competing priorities. This causes a negative kind of stress. Good stress leads to growth, while bad stress leads to burnout. Imagine if I drew a dot on the wall and asked you to walk toward it. It's a clear, easy path and you know exactly where to go. Now, imagine if I drew two dots on the wall that weren't close together and told you to walk toward them. You'll be stumped and end up walking nowhere because you don't know which dot to walk toward. This quickly becomes confusing. Having competing goals delays progress. Before you know it, you're spreading yourself thin, trying to do too much at once. You struggle with consistency, which leads to discouragement and lowers your motivation. It all ends the same way: you burn out.

The way to avoid this is to cultivate laser focus. Laser focus requires prioritizing tasks and managing your time. I actively use two methods to help with both. The first, which I cannot live without, is the Eisenhower Matrix. This tool helps with decision making. Sometimes you may struggle with understanding what's critical to prioritize and what isn't. The Eisenhower Matrix helps distinguish tasks that are important, not important, urgent, and not urgent. It splits tasks into four boxes, prioritizing which tasks you should focus on first and which you should delegate or delete.

THE EISENHOWER MATRIX

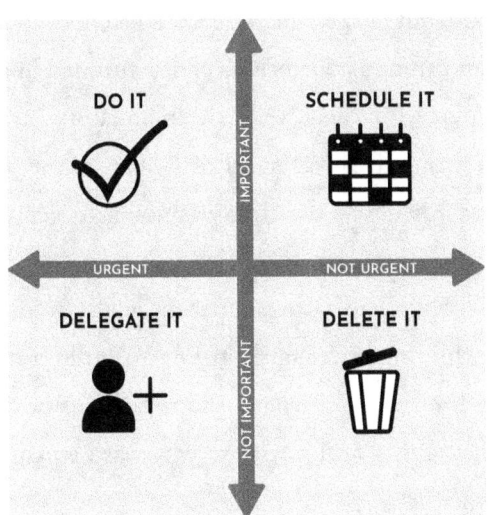

Laser focus requires time management, otherwise you'll get distracted and lose focus. The second method that helps with this is time boxing. This involves allocating a specific amount of time for certain tasks, and during that time, all you're allowed to work on is the task at hand. If you allocate a large time box for a task on your schedule, you have to be realistic about your concentration span, so take breaks every half hour. This is very similar to the Pomodoro Technique, and it works exceptionally well for completing long tasks.

In my early career, I was organizing a statewide tour for the governor for his reelection campaign. Amid this incredible whirlwind, I got nervous about what came after the election. My mind pondered a million questions. Was I doing enough with my life? Would this career lead me as far as I wanted to go? I thought of taking on a second college degree. Many people around me were going to law school and, out of the blue, I decided I should, too. As the campaign came to a victorious end, I enrolled in a preparation course for the LSAT, the mandatory law school entrance exam. This was never really part of my plan, but somehow, I believed that if I was going to get a second higher level degree, why not a legal degree?

Suddenly I had two competing goals: going to law school, while simultaneously trying to build a career in politics. The truth was that I didn't need to be a lawyer for the field I was working in, so why was I embarking on this new path?

Over the next few months, I rigorously prepared myself to take the LSAT. However, my performance at work began to suffer because I was trying to tackle two different paths. The reality was I wasn't succeeding in either pursuit. My practice test scores were improving, but I didn't have the time to make the kind of improvements I needed to attend a top ten law school. Competing goals came at the expense of my professional aspirations. I didn't want to practice law full time; I wanted to work in the political field.

Eventually, I admitted to myself that I'd reached a level of burnout I hadn't thought possible. I was unmotivated, irritable, and unhappy to the point where I didn't want to be on any path. I took the LSAT and did well, but realized that law school would divert me from building a career in the field I was passionate about. While I'm sure I would have found some level of success as a lawyer, it wasn't in my plan.

By clearing that unnecessary goal, I paved the way for immense success in the field I worked in, leading me to become the top one percent in my field.

What transpired later in life continues to amaze me. As I grew my client base, I began referring the legal side of my work to a lawyer friend of mine, whom I greatly admire. He was working at a top fifty law firm, and one day, as we sat down to collaborate, we realized how much work we were doing together and decided to open a law firm that incorporated consulting. This is how I ended up cofounding a law firm in addition to my consultancy. In the end, I got to have the best of both worlds. This would have never been possible if I hadn't become laser focused on my goal eleven years prior. Life unfolds in mysterious ways when we do our part. Do your part and get focused.

II. STRIVING FOR PERFECTION

The root of all evil is perfection. Yes, I know this is a controversial opinion. Get over it and stop trying to make everything perfect. It's important that you understand why I'm saying this. Everything in your life needs to be considered through a cost-benefit analysis. It sounds overly strategic, but you must learn to be strategic. If it takes an extra hour to make something perfect, consider that you could have spent that time on your next task or something more lucrative. Accept your product as final, even though it's not perfect, and move on. You'll find that when you do a cost-benefit analysis on everything, it rarely pays off to dedicate that extra precious time to perfection. Good enough is good enough. Good enough gets you to the next step, and the next step is progress, and progress is how we accomplish things in life. Don't allow yourself to get stuck because you're obsessed with perfection.

Perfection is a myth. You'll never be one hundred percent perfect—neither will your work, health, or body.

It's impossible, merely a fantasy. So, stop trying to live up to unreasonable self-imposed expectations. Learn to love your imperfections. Some people wait their entire lives for the "perfect" time to start something. Well, I hate to break it to you, but the perfect time doesn't exist. Just do it. Perfection exists in imperfection. Striving for perfection leads to overthinking, procrastinating, leaving tasks unfinished, and hindering your creativity.

As someone with a busy schedule, I rarely have time to dedicate to extra activities. I always prioritize tasks tied to my mental, emotional, and financial growth. After getting engaged right before the COVID-19 pandemic began, I was waiting for the right time to get married. As I mentioned, there is no right time. With lockdowns and restrictions, it was nearly impossible to plan a destination wedding I envisioned. I delayed any attempt to plan something. Finally, I got serious and got to work. First, I selected a destination and the venue, and then I did the smartest thing I could—I hired a wedding planner.

However, even with the planner's help, months went by because I was incredibly busy with work and kept putting off our discussions. I was waiting for the perfect time to start planning. This procrastination, fueled by my desire for perfection, led to full panic mode when I realized I had only four months until the wedding, and I hadn't even sent out invites yet. Nothing would be perfect, so I gave the planner explicit instructions to make everything beautiful and white with lots of white roses. I told her I didn't need to be consulted; I only wanted confirmation of the final decisions she made.

At the end of the day, there were no perfect wine glasses or table napkins. I needed to shift from striving for perfection to being realistic. I even waited a whole year to find the perfect dance instructor to help us choreograph the perfect wedding dance. In the end, I choreographed it with an instructor in my hotel room three days before the wedding. My pursuit of perfection led to some serious last-minute stress, but guess what—I pulled it off and let go of the ridiculous notion that everything had to be perfect. In the guests' eyes, the entire wedding was perfect. I will never forget how I pulled it off, and what still makes me laugh is how my desire for perfection almost destroyed the entire event. Never again, I told myself. Good enough is good enough!

Striving for perfection often leads to delayed progress, so don't fall prey to this.

III. GET USED TO REJECTION

Rejection ranks among life's most difficult experiences. Humans are wired in such a way that when we face rejection, we endure immense suffering. We have a fundamental need to belong, as social acceptance is vital to our survival. Our brains process rejection similarly to how they process physical pain, and there's a great deal of research on this subject.

Refusing to accept rejection hinders the ability to execute a plan and make progress. Focusing too long on rejection can lead to discouragement and depression, and often, we don't try again. This is the "loser" mentality creeping in. Don't fall into this trap.

It's all about perspective. Adapting your mindset can help you view rejection differently, which leads to processing it differently. Rejection is a good thing. In fact, it's a great thing, as it makes us resilient. Stop making a big deal out of being rejected for a job, a boyfriend, or in any other scenario. Who cares! Embrace rejection as a sign to move on to the next opportunity. I used to get down on myself when things didn't work out the way I had anticipated. However, I soon realized that after every rejection, the heavens opened up, and when one door closed, a window opened. There was always another opportunity on the horizon, but it's hard to see it if you're still feeling down about the initial rejection.

Rejection is redirection. Embrace the fact that something isn't meant for you. Rejection is a sign of that. The more basketballs you shoot, the more baskets you make, so keep shooting. Don't quit just because you missed a shot. Stop taking rejection so personally—sometimes it isn't about you. After all, rejection happens to everyone. If you remain persistent, rejection will only be temporary. If not, you'll never be able to execute your life plan or reach your goals.

I have faced rejection more times than I can count, and I've learned to stop taking it personally. I have a rule: if I'm feeling down about something like being rejected, I allow myself one day to sulk. On that day, I eat whatever I want and allow myself to feel however I want to feel. The next morning, I wake up as if nothing happened and get back to my regular routine. Your ability to move on is what makes you a success. You won't be everyone's cup of tea, so don't take it personally.

Before I started my own company in 2014, I was up for a big job at the Chamber of Commerce, and I was excited about the opportunity. It came from a contact within my professional network. The final decision was between me and another woman I knew. My final interview went so well, I was dancing on my way to the car, believing I had the job. I was so happy I even high-fived the parking attendant on my way out. Imagine my shock when I got an email a few days later informing me that I did not get the job.

That day, I bought a box of Krispy Kreme doughnuts and ate them all while I sulked on my sofa. The next morning, I woke up feeling horribly ill after devouring those doughnuts. After a long shower to shake off my disappointment, I realized I could either recalibrate and get back to figuring out what was next or drown in victimhood. I circled back to some of my professional contacts to find out if I could help with a project or if anyone was hiring. To my surprise, within a few hours, I was offered a three-month contract. My contact suggested I open my own consulting company and take on the consulting portion of the work. I was blown away. Why hadn't I thought of that sooner?

That rejection led me to open my consultancy, which I worked hard to grow over the following years before merging with another firm. In hindsight, that rejection was the best thing that ever happened to me. I was being rejected for a reason. It was a message from the heavens that I was destined for more. Accepting the temporary rejection allowed me to open another chapter in my life—one that led to true success.

Years later, at a networking happy hour, I ran into the contact who had referred me to that job. He asked me what I was working on, and the satisfaction of telling him about the company I had built was priceless. He was blown away.

Accepting rejection forces us to realign our plans, and sometimes that's exactly what the doctor ordered. Adjust, keep building, and keep executing.

CHAPTER SEVEN LESSONS

Not following through on your plans can prevent you from reaching your goals and realizing your vision for life. Execution is essential; without it, your dreams remain just those—dreams.

1. Importance of Execution
- Execution turns plans into reality.
- Assess yourself regularly to ensure your actions align with your goals. Monthly evaluations help identify whether your efforts are leading you to success or merely keeping you busy.

2. Realignment and Growth
- Comfort can hinder growth. Leaving a familiar job may be scary, but it can lead to better opportunities.
- Self-assessment reveals when you're off track and helps redirect your efforts toward meaningful progress.

3. Setting Too Many Goals
- Having too many goals can lead to confusion, becoming overwhelmed, and burnout.
- Use prioritization tools like the Eisenhower Matrix to focus your efforts effectively.

- Time management techniques, such as time boxing, can improve focus.

4. Striving for Perfection
- Perfectionism can stall progress. A cost-benefit analysis helps prioritize tasks without getting bogged down in details.
- Accept that "good enough" often leads to progress. Embrace imperfections as part of the journey.

5. Dealing with Rejection
- Rejection is a natural part of life, and learning to cope with it is crucial for moving forward.
- Change your perspective to view rejection as redirection. Each setback can open new doors.
- Allow brief moments of disappointment, but quickly return to identifying new opportunities.

Facing the truth about your progress and focusing on fewer goals can lead to substantial advancements. Embrace imperfection, manage your time effectively, and learn to handle rejection. These strategies are essential for executing your plans, overcoming obstacles, and achieving your aspirations.

CHAPTER SEVEN EXERCISE

Monthly Assessment

Assess whether you're walking toward one of your goals or if you're simply taking the route that looks easiest.

Are you on the path you want to be on right now?

What have you accomplished this month?

How does that align with your goal?

If it doesn't align with your goal, how will you realign it?

Prioritize Your Tasks

Laser focus requires prioritizing your tasks and time management.

What tasks do you need to work on this month?

Follow the Eisenhower Matrix to distinguish which of these tasks are important, not important, urgent, or not urgent. Categorize your tasks into the four groups to prioritize which to tackle, delegate, or delete.

CHAPTER 8

FIGURE IT OUT

Become familiar with the unfamiliar. Not knowing how to do something is the rocket fuel for success. The more you find yourself in situations where you don't know how to do something, the more you're forced to learn. Nothing familiar or comfortable contributes to growth. Personal growth and reaching the level of success where you feel satisfied and fulfilled requires stepping out of your comfort zone. People achieve nothing in their comfort zone. I've spent my entire life living outside my comfort zone. While I dread the feeling of the unknown, it's necessary to be successful.

Your most uncomfortable experiences build your character. This is where development and learning occur. The truth is, you doubt yourself and feel scared to step out of your comfort zone, but remember that those watching on the sidelines are terrified of your potential, knowing that if you reach your full potential, you'll be a force to be reckoned with.

Not knowing how to do something is normal, so get used to that feeling. I've been learning throughout my entire career, and I'm not ashamed of it. Part of stepping out of your comfort zone is learning something new. Figure it out as you go. There is no other way but through it. The only person coming to save you, teach you, and guide you is you.

Learning as you go entails adopting an adaptive approach, which starts with being thrown into a task. This requires action—take that extra project on at work even if you don't really know how you'll execute it. The challenge will force you to learn something. Learning as you go means you won't be perfect, and you'll certainly make mistakes. Get used to it! There's nothing wrong with making mistakes. Learning as you go is a game of trial and error. Don't allow a mistake to defeat you or make you quit. Quitters never succeed. The only things you should quit are bad habits.

If you don't know how to do something, seek help and ask someone who does. This is why your professional network is so critical to success. Someone will know exactly how to help you. While this is stressful at first, remember that stress forces you to improve performance and sharpen your focus. Overcoming stress provides a sense of accomplishment, which fosters resilience. With each new project, task, or venture you conquer, you become more and more confident in your abilities. This may be an unpopular opinion, but I believe stress isn't always negative—it catalyzes growth. So, the next time you feel stressed or overwhelmed and have no idea what you're doing, embrace it. On the other side lies victory, growth, and resilience.

I experienced this firsthand while working on my first congressional election campaign. My candidate was a member of my state's General Assembly and served as the Majority Whip, which is a leadership position in the ruling party that helps unite the party and garner votes for key legislative bills. He was an influential individual, and working for him was a strategic decision. Even if he didn't win the election, he had the best professional network of any candidate, and I planned to take full advantage of it.

I had no previous campaign experience aside from volunteer work. I was fresh out of university, and a newbie in the political arena. One thing was certain: I knew I wanted it, and I was going to work for it. I joined the campaign and worked as a scheduler, managing the candidate's schedule. It was an entry-level job, but that didn't deter me. If I applied myself, I'd get promoted. I had never managed anyone's schedule, so I learned as I went. I went the extra mile every day by showing up on weekends to knock on doors with my candidate, organizing events, and fundraising. I knew nothing about any of these tasks.

It was uncomfortable, to say the least, but pushing myself out of my comfort zone worked because I learned about all aspects of a political campaign and got promoted! I was excited to take on a new role in the campaign.

What I didn't know was that I'd face my first real test in the first week. *Knock Knock*—it was the campaign manager. "Vlada, I need you to do a press release for the upcoming opening of the campaign office," he said.

I smiled and replied, "Yes, of course, Tom. I'll get it to you today." The door closed, and I felt mortified. I had never written a press release. What on earth did I even learn in college? I had no clue where to even start. One part of me was angry with myself for pretending as if I knew what Tom was asking of me, while the other part of me remembered that if I wanted to get somewhere in life, I had to figure it out. How hard could it be? It wasn't rocket science. The only way to a solution was straight through the problem, not around it.

I started reading about the basic tenets of writing a press release online and looked at dozens of samples. After an hour of research, I started writing, and before I knew it, I was done. I read it over and was impressed with my work. It sounded legitimate, so I formatted everything properly and printed it.

Tom's brow furrowed intently as he read it between sips of coffee. I was getting nervous, but I reminded myself that I needed to project confidence. When he was done, he looked up and said, "Great job, kid! You really do know how to do it all. You'll go far."

Wow! I was shocked; it was my first attempt, and I nailed it. Slam dunk!

The next day, the release appeared in the newspaper and on many other sites. The power of pushing myself out of my comfort zone was unbelievable. I learned something valuable that day, and now I laugh when I look back because I have since written or reviewed hundreds of press releases, and it all started with an inexperienced girl who knew nothing but was willing to give it a try. I figured it out, and so can you. Failure isn't an option, and not trying shouldn't be an option either. The next time you don't know how to do something and you feel terrified at failing, follow these steps:

1. Tell yourself it isn't that hard.
2. Teach yourself about the subject or task.
3. Try it, and if you fail, try again.

Approach anything with the perspective of "I just need to try it out." Commit to becoming more familiar with the subject and how people usually get it done and give it a try. Eventually, you'll find success. If you start with an open mind, miracles will happen. However, if you approach it with fear and tell yourself that you've never done this and that, it will be impossible. You'll just program that computer inside your head to not bother trying.

I. IDENTIFY OPPORTUNITIES

Part of figuring it out is learning to identify opportunities. Few of us are wired to see opportunities everywhere we look. Most often, we miss the ones right in front of us. I experienced this working on a campaign for the former president of the United Nations General Assembly. He was running for president in the Balkans. It was the most miserable campaign I have ever worked on in my life. His team was impossible to deal with. They had no clue what they were doing, and they didn't take direction well. I felt trapped in a horrible campaign, and half the time, the candidate disregarded me, saying he couldn't take me seriously because I was "too pretty." Which was flattering, but also incredibly insulting.

The silver lining was that he had great contacts, but I had no idea how to leverage them properly. It was still early in my political consulting career, and I hadn't yet harnessed a success mentality. I considered how I could turn this opportunity into a success and realized that, even if we dropped him as a client, I needed to make something out of that connection. His impressive contacts surrounded me, and I knew I should take advantage of that.

One individual, John, always seemed especially supportive of my team and me. When he invited us to dinner, I had to make a good impression. There was so much I could learn from him, as he had worked for the former president of the country. He had gotten his political start early in life, leading a revolution of the youth.

We began communicating regularly, and one day I asked him for career guidance, knowing he was well connected and could help me grow as a young political strategist and expand my network. Eventually, my team and I quit the campaign and dropped the client. The candidate had become unmanageable. I left the project and the country but remained in touch with John. One day, he messaged me to say he had recommended me for a leadership program in Germany, which consisted of young people across the European political spectrum. He himself was an alumnus of the program. I was pleasantly surprised that he had thought of me and was eager to be selected. John warned me that I'd be one of very few politically conservative candidates. The opportunity was a golden one, so I submitted my documents and awaited the final decision. I was accepted!

That summer, I spent two weeks in Germany with some of the youngest and brightest minds from dozens of countries around the world. Overnight, I expanded my network by a million. Sharing my conservative views with individuals from liberal European governments wasn't always comfortable, but I enjoyed the dialogue. Those two weeks in Germany tested my relationship boundaries. Every evening, we'd get together for a post-dinner night cap in someone's private room. However, that wasn't how I wanted a professional network to perceive me. It was challenging not to cross professional lines, but I remained disciplined. While everyone else drank until one in the morning, I took a hot shower and then read, and woke up early for a workout and to review the agenda for the day. I consistently put my best foot forward.

Every day, someone from the group asked me how I managed to keep it together, which made me laugh. I wouldn't have been so well put together if I drank all night. Impressions matter. Once you seize a good opportunity, don't mess it up by being unprofessional. To this day, I'm still in touch with the alumni. They've been a tremendous asset in my work, and I truly value their professional expertise and alternative viewpoints. I owe it all to the fact that I connected with John. It was an opportunity I seized, and it paid off in ways I could not have expected.

II. PUT YOURSELF OUT THERE

If I could bet a million dollars, I would wager that you're not putting yourself out there enough. What are you hiding from? Step up to the plate and get it done. Why aren't you pushing yourself to speak up more often in meetings? Why do you cower in the face of an issue? Why aren't you taking chances and seizing opportunities to prove yourself when they're right in front of you? Get out into the world, be visible and accessible to the right people, and take the initiative.

If you dare to tell me you don't need to prove yourself to anyone, prepare for a slap in the face. Of course, you need to prove yourself. You'll need to do so for the rest of your life. I'm a multi-millionaire with six residences across four continents, dozens of cars, and nine companies, and I'm still proving myself every day. Think of proving yourself as an opportunity to make a lasting impression. This doesn't mean you should flaunt being the smartest person in the room. In fact, you should never be the smartest person in the room. If you are, you're in the wrong room. Part of putting yourself out there is finding new rooms that offer learning opportunities.

If an opportunity to take extra initiative comes up at work, why wouldn't you? By putting yourself out there and being open to doing more, you'll gain more and elevate to the next level.

On a warm day in Tel Aviv, as the sun shone brightly through the stunning five-star hotel lobby, my business partner and I were sitting with Samuel, a professional contact—someone who regularly brought us into countries for high-level projects. I wasn't overly focused on the meeting, rather, I was much more eager to enjoy an afternoon cocktail in the beautiful weather. Samuel asked my business partner to come to South Sudan; however, the dates didn't work for my business partner.

In that moment, I realized I could passively move on or volunteer myself to go in his place. A trip to South Sudan could yield business contacts and I could learn something new. An internal conflict was raging inside me. Was I crazy? Why did I need to go to the war-torn streets of South Sudan? It wasn't safe. South Sudan is the world's youngest country, and it has faced significant challenges since gaining its independence in 2011. It has been ravaged by civil war, and its infrastructure is severely underdeveloped. Despite the peace agreement, violence periodically flares up.

Success mentality requires you to see opportunities where others don't. It forces you to view things through a different lens. Where many see political instability, governance issues, and poverty, I saw something completely different. I saw a new African nation striving to develop and needing guidance. I saw a country rich in oil but needing help to develop its infrastructure. It was raw and a bit rough around the edges, but I recognized the opportunity and found purpose in being able to help a country that could impact millions of lives.

"Those dates work great for me, Samuel. I can accompany you on the trip," I stated. My partner looked over at me in shock. A young, five-foot-four, 123-pound blonde was volunteering to step foot in South Sudan. My business partner was stunned.

"Are you sure?" he asked cautiously.

"Yes, I'm sure," I stated firmly. Samuel looked amused and asked if I was scared, but I wasn't. I was excited and eager. They couldn't believe it. I was seizing the opportunity and putting myself out there. It would be an experience of a lifetime—a privilege of the highest kind. How many people could say they had an opportunity like that?

A few weeks passed, and before I knew it, I was in Dubai boarding a private jet to Juba, South Sudan, the capital. Exhaustion from weeks of travel prior caught up with me and I fell fast asleep on the flight. The flight attendant woke me up one hour before we landed. I freshened up and put on a gray suit; it was too late to have regrets now. It was really happening. Was I getting in over my head by going into a war-torn nation? Would I even be safe?

As the plane began its initial descent, I faced the reality of where I was landing. The pilots weren't getting permission to land. In fact, there was no communication from the tower at all, which made me wonder if another conflict had broken out.

Samuel instructed the pilot to land anyway, and I wondered if he was serious. It turned out he was, and he instructed me to get with the program and buckle up. As we touched down, I noticed a line of soldiers in military uniforms with maroon berets and what looked like AK-47s strapped over their shoulders.

"Well, you've done it now," I thought to myself. Maybe I had pushed myself a little too far out of my comfort zone. I realized that nothing would kill me faster than my own mind. There was no need to stress about what was out of my control.

The plane door opened, and the steps were brought down. Samuel and his business partner smiled and said, "You go first."

Were they serious? Was I the sacrificial lamb? I looked at them, smiling, "Please tell me these guys are expecting us and are on our side."

He laughed. "I'm not sure, but we're about to find out."

Full of confidence, I was the first to step out of the plane, my black stilettos clinking down the steps. Immediately, I was greeted by a man in military uniform. I looked him dead in the eye and spoke with authority, asking where protocol and security were, and it worked. In a flash, protocol officers and security surrounded me, welcoming me like a queen.

I had incredible meetings across various levels of government and learned a great deal over those few days. My visit to South Sudan was one of the greatest experiences in my professional life, all because I put myself out there and spotted an opportunity where many people didn't.

Let this example serve as a reminder that nothing is ever as scary or uncomfortable as it seems. Put yourself out there, learn to see opportunity in everything, and seize the moment. You'll thank me later. Don't wait for an invitation. No one invited me on that trip—I invited myself. Don't ask, just do. Get out there and get it done. You'll be glad you did.

III. NAVIGATING UNCHARTED TERRITORY

So, you've put yourself out there, yet you have no idea what you're doing. Well, congratulations! You've already gone farther than half the population. Entering uncharted territory requires trusting your instincts and relying on your gut feelings, but it also requires doing your research. I cannot stress this enough. Ask people for advice and gather as much information on the subject as you can. You're not the first person in the world to find yourself in this situation.

In 2016, I was working on a project in Azerbaijan, Western Asia, where I managed a large team. I loved working there and was confident in myself, my team, and our joint ability to execute our plans. I had a great working relationship with our local partners and, while this region of the world was relatively new to me, I spoke one of the local languages and adapted rather well. We made all the preparations and executed all aspects of our plan.

Election day came, and the media stormed the grand hall where our team was processing data. "What are they doing here?" I asked myself, knowing it was way too early for media. Before I knew it, cameras were in my face. I had prepared for all scenarios of our project, but I had never prepared for media because I wasn't in charge of that. There was a designated spokesperson responsible for media, but he was nowhere to be found.

Panicking, I frantically messaged him, only to find out he was at the studio doing a segment for live TV. "You'll have to do the media interviews," he said. "I have to go. Good luck!"

What??? I wasn't ready for that. I had spoken to the press a few times, but not on camera. I wasn't ready to give seven different interviews on camera. Well, I had no choice. In a situation like that, the worst thing you can do is appear unsure of yourself. Fake it till you make it, they say. I don't care what anyone tells you—every successful person faked knowing how to do something until it became familiar.

I stood up defiantly, gathered all the media, and told them we would begin interviews in twenty minutes. They set up the cameras so we could conduct individual interviews before the larger press conference. They scurried about like little squirrels following my strict instructions. While they were occupied, I gathered a few members of my team, including one who'd worked closely with multiple United States presidents in the past. I asked what points she felt I needed to cover in the interview. She handed me a breakdown of what we were doing that day and what I could highlight in the interviews. Life-saver! I thought. The rest of my team offered a few pointers, and I was off to the races.

"You're going to do great!" I told myself, giving myself the ultimate pep talk. As I walked toward the first camera, I realized the local staff members, who were predominantly younger females, were watching me. I was an inspiration to them. They had no idea I had so little experience in front of the camera, but I would not let them down. I smiled at them, becoming a bit emotional. I wondered how many times in their lives they had entered uncharted territory and felt alone and unsure of themselves. They saw me as someone who had it all together. Yet, they were the ones who gave me that extra bit of confidence I needed, and they didn't even know it.

It was showtime! One TV station at a time, I got up in front of the camera and gave great interviews. In the end, there was nothing to fear in that uncharted territory. I had garnered enough self-trust to put myself out there, I figured it out, and I delivered. After the one-on-one interviews, I did a brief press conference in front of all the cameras. By that point, I was moving forward full steam.

As the cameras were being packed away, the young women approached me to take pictures. They had admired me, but what they didn't know was that I admired them far more. Their belief in me moved mountains. It became one of the most special moments in my professional career.

Every few years when I return to Azerbaijan for work, a new team of young women takes pictures with me after media appearances. I tell them they can do anything they set their minds to, and I share the story of how it was women like them who gave me the confidence I needed to navigate unchartered waters. The most amazing part of this experience is that I did so well with those first press appearances that I've since become the most requested interviewee in every project I've been involved with.

Do not be afraid to enter uncharted territory. Believe it or not, it usually works out. You grow immensely when you learn to identify opportunities, put yourself out there, and navigate through situations where you lack experience. Nothing can substitute the kind of growth you gain from life experiences.

CHAPTER EIGHT LESSONS

Understanding how to navigate unfamiliar situations is essential for personal growth and success. Stepping outside of your comfort zone is necessary for gaining new skills and experiences, which build character and resilience.

1. Learning from the Unknown

- Not knowing how to do something is a common experience. It's essential to embrace this feeling to foster growth.
- Comfort zones don't lead to personal or professional development. True success lies outside these zones.
- Character and learning grow in uncomfortable situations.

2. Learning as You Go

- Adopt an adaptive approach by taking on tasks even if you lack expertise.
- Expect to make mistakes; they're a natural part of the learning process. Use them as opportunities for improvement.
- Build a professional network for support and guidance in unfamiliar tasks.

3. Stress and Growth

- While stress can be overwhelming, it often enhances performance and sharpens focus.
- Overcoming stress leads to accomplishments and increased confidence in your abilities.

4. Identifying Opportunities

- It's essential to recognize and seize opportunities, even in challenging circumstances.
- Making connections, such as engaging with influential individuals, can lead to significant opportunities.

5. Putting Yourself Out There

- Taking risks and being visible in professional situations is crucial.

6. Navigating Uncharted Territory

- Entering unfamiliar situations requires trusting your instincts, gathering information, and seeking advice.
- Embracing the unknown often results in growth and valuable life lessons.

Venturing into unfamiliar situations can be daunting, yet it significantly boosts personal and professional growth. By identifying opportunities, taking risks, and learning from mistakes, you develop resilience and confidence. Embrace what feels uncomfortable, seek knowledge, and recognize the power of seizing opportunities to grow and thrive.

CHAPTER 9

"NO" IS NOT AN ANSWER

Those who know me know I never accept "no" for an answer. In professional negotiations, no never means no. Accepting the answer "no" when you want something is tantamount to accepting that you'll never get what you're after. Accepting "no" signifies defeat and holds you back at every turn. When you concede, you settle for less than what you're capable of achieving. If you stop at the first "no," you get only what you accept, and usually it's less than you deserve. This acceptance stifles your growth, and unless you push past it, you're not overcoming an obstacle, which ultimately hinders your resilience. A "no" prevents you from getting places in life, so train yourself not to accept a "no."

In a business context, "no" is never a final answer; it's merely a stepping stone to a "yes." This is the perspective I want you to adopt from now on. Consider "no" a starting point for conversation, dialogue, negotiations, and the re-evaluation of circumstances. Instead of viewing "no" as a refusal, see it as a golden opportunity to reevaluate, improve, and prepare for something much better. If I could tell you the number of times I've been told "no," you'd be shocked. This has become a game for me; every "no" is a challenge I look forward to.

You may have noticed that I included the context of a business environment because it's essential to understand that when it comes to personal boundaries, "no" means "no." The twenty-first century has fostered a culture of consent, where everyone is entitled to feel safe and empowered to express their boundaries. In a personal context, you must deeply respect and honor a firm "no."

When Russia invaded Ukraine in 2022, I was determined to do everything in my power to help. The humanitarian toll became so large it was unbearable. I wanted to start a nonprofit organization to send humanitarian aid into the country, so I turned to other nonprofit organizations for advice. At every turn, I was told it was impossible to get a nonprofit organization up and running quickly, and that getting a tax exemption in such a short period would be nearly impossible. As deflated as I felt, I continued calling everyone I knew, including lawyers familiar with the process. Most of them told me the same thing: no. When someone said "no," it meant they weren't experienced enough to do it, not that it couldn't be done.

I hired a lawyer from one of the top fifty law firms in the United States who told me it wasn't only possible but would be done quickly. Within four days of the war breaking out in Ukraine, my nonprofit organization was founded, and within two weeks, I had all the documentation for the tax-exempt status. What was impossible for someone else wasn't impossible for me. What was a "no" from ninety percent of the people I had spoken to was a "yes" for the right experienced professional.

I wouldn't have done anything if I had gotten discouraged and stopped trying. By the organization's third year of operations, it had delivered millions of dollars' worth of aid to Ukraine and helped millions of people in a war zone. The nonprofit organization has received endorsements from Ukrainian celebrities and garnered bipartisan support from former congressmen and senators in the United States. None of this would have been possible if I had accepted the answer "no."

I. KNOW WHO TO ASK

The issue we often face is that we don't know who to approach for help. Asking the wrong person often leads to a "no." You must be strategic. Target someone knowledgeable about the subject area and best suited to help. However, don't be fooled; the best person for the task may not be the best person to approach. If this person is going to be a hardliner and give you a "no"—whether it's for a reference, involvement in a project, or access to a professional network—they are definitely not the best person to go to.

The person you want to target isn't necessarily going to be the most knowledgeable; instead, it's the person from whom you can almost ensure a "yes" or at least build the pathway to a "yes." This concept is crucial to understand. If you approach someone for a reference simply because they're the best-known option on your list, it doesn't mean they'll give you a good reference. If they seem hesitant at first and then reluctantly agree, that is not your person. Go for the low-hanging fruit, not the most juicy apple at the top of the tree. The low-hanging fruit can yield quick results, and they're more likely to give you a "yes" or at least be negotiable enough to get there.

At work, if you want to ask for a raise, it would not be wise to go to someone at the top who doesn't seem impressed or respectful of you. Instead, build a coalition of people right below them who may have a more favorable attitude toward you. Target someone in this group who has some influence and strike up a conversation to test the waters before making the official ask. Testing the waters is critical for understanding where you stand in various situations, which can help you mitigate a "no,"

I was once up for a nationwide job with a political organization that has a national footprint. They were looking for a national director, and I was the youngest candidate for the job, and the only woman. Everyone at the headquarters in Washington, DC, was supportive of me. I was told I was the top candidate for the job.

A female politician in my state was heavily involved in the organization and had significant influence over the board, so I thought she'd be the right person to approach. I could have gone to other board members who were easier to reach, but she and I were from the same state, so I truly believed she would be supportive.

I searched far and wide for her contact information and finally got her direct number and invited her for a coffee to discuss the position and ask for support. She had met me before on numerous occasions at various events and knew all the politicians I had worked for. Imagine my surprise when I met her and sensed her hesitation to support me. In fact, that conversation has replayed in my mind ever since. "Aren't you a little young for such a big role? Don't you think you're aiming a little high? Maybe you should start somewhere more entry-level or mid-level."

Coming from someone who hadn't finished college but had worked at some of the highest levels in our state, I wouldn't have expected those words to come out of her mouth. I was a bit shocked because I had a college degree, experience working for the governor of our state, and had led numerous campaigns for congressmen and senators. I hardly considered myself unqualified. Her hesitation revealed everything I needed to know. She claimed she wasn't supporting anyone else and didn't know any other candidates, which further alarmed me. It meant she was a woman who didn't want to support other women.

I dug down to the core of her issue and asked what her hesitation was. There it was in all its glory: "I didn't move up that fast in my career, so you should take your time," she said. The problem was that I had made a grave miscalculation by approaching her. I knew men from other states who were on the board and would have supported me, but instead of going for the quick, easy targets, I thought it would be better to seek support from someone from my state, especially a woman. I couldn't have been more wrong. Ultimately, she was the deciding vote on the board, and I didn't get the position.

What I gained was a lifetime of wisdom. Be strategic, plan your target, and know who to approach. I felt vindicated when she attempted to run for another political office in my state and sought support. Many people from her camp came to talk to me, and I told them I couldn't support a woman who didn't support women. She hasn't pursued any further political endeavors. I didn't blame her; I blamed myself for not being wiser.

II. FEARING "NO"

Fear can be one of the most crippling factors that prevent us from taking action. It's the foundation of self-doubt, making you question yourself in many aspects. Fear often manifests itself in different ways, such as anxiety. When you fear a negative response, your anxiety kicks in, and you begin to imagine all the negative outcomes, which drains your energy. Do not fear something that does not yet exist. Fearing a "no" answer is something we've all faced. Don't feel ashamed if a negative answer triggers anxiety. This makes you human; however, you need to become superhuman and stop fearing what hasn't even happened.

You can rewire your brain by training yourself to always go for the ask. The worst thing that can happen is that someone says "no," and there's nothing scary about that. Doing a cost-benefit analysis shows that you gain more by trying than not trying at all. We rarely realize what we're missing out on by not trying or asking.

I was working for one of the largest public affairs firms in Washington, DC, and had built up a great book of business. They hired me to fill a mid-level position, but based on my revenue numbers, I should have qualified to move up to a senior position. I wanted to bring this up with the managing partner, but kept putting it off for fear that it might look desperate. Instead, I waited for the yearly evaluation, where surely no one could overlook my performance and revenue.

It took place less than six months later, and I was excited about what I was sure would be a serious promotion. I was traveling for work and couldn't attend the review in person, so I had to participate via video conference. The entire review focused on how impressive I was, how I had superior evaluations from other employees, how my numbers were incredible, and that I was an asset to the firm. I waited eagerly for the announcement, but it never came. What came instead was a huge company bonus, almost as large as my salary. I was thrilled, but what happened to my promotion? The numbers were there, and I knew I had met the necessary revenue targets.

I feared it was the wrong time to ask during such a positive call, so I didn't. After the call, while heading to a client dinner, I became enraged with myself. A hot flash came over me at the thought that I couldn't put on my big-girl pants and just ask the freaking question: why wasn't I promoted? Why did I let fear set in? What was I afraid of?

I immediately took out my cell phone and texted the senior partner. I thanked him for a wonderful evaluation and asked if I could access my revenue markers, explaining that I was sure I would be promoted and wanted to understand if there was an issue I wasn't aware of. He seemed a bit surprised, but thanked me for bringing it up and said he would check himself.

It wasn't so bad, so I wasn't sure why I had been so hesitant before. I tucked my phone away and told myself I wouldn't stress about it anymore until after dinner. As I wrapped up my client dinner, I opened my phone to find a message that read, "I'm not sure how we missed it, but the numbers are there, and you'll be promoted. Congratulations!" It was really that simple, yet it had taken me months to get to that point.

That day, I vowed never to doubt myself for fear of an outcome. You should not doubt yourself either. Ask for a promotion, ask to be included, ask for support, ask for the reference, and ask for help. You'll see that you have the world to gain and very little to lose.

III. YOU ARE NOT A VICTIM

The most important thing I could ever tell you is: DON'T BE A VICTIM. In life, you have the option of becoming a victor or a victim. Often, when faced with situations where we are told "no," we slip into a victim mentality. We shift blame on others, claiming they blocked us from reaching our goals or that if it weren't for them, we'd be much further along. Victimhood is dangerous and can quickly turn into a permanent mentality. It prevents personal growth and traps you in a vicious cycle of bitterness and resentment, reducing your motivation to strive for more.

Being stuck in a victim mentality means you cannot embrace the success mentality. Accepting the answer "no" turns you into a victim faster than anything else. Do not allow this to happen. I never allow myself to be a victim in any situation. Instead, empower yourself by learning to push beyond boundaries to get to where you want to be. There's always a pathway to "yes." You can empower yourself by taking responsibility for your successes and failures. Taking responsibility forces you to take control and tackle challenges head-on. Focus on solutions instead of problems and take action. Surround yourself with the right people who will help you get past the "noes" in life. Empowering yourself will give you the control, resilience, and confidence you need to keep trying and avoid falling into victimhood.

I attended a public high school where I didn't fit in with any group. I didn't fit in with the wealthy preppy kids because I wasn't from a wealthy family. While I tried to dress the part, they knew I wasn't like them. I didn't fit in with the Hispanic immigrants either, since I didn't look like them, didn't speak Spanish, and wasn't culturally similar. To succeed in high school, I needed to break into a social clique, or I'd be left behind to die in the social world of high school. My high school had 1,300 students, so surely I could find a clique to be a part of. Sports seemed to be the bridge for everyone. If you had some talent in the world of sports, it didn't matter if you were rich or poor. People who played sports together also had their own cliques.

I dated a guy in high school, Nelson, who was on the swim team. He was an incredible swimmer and should have gone for the Olympic trials. So, I decided to join the swim team. I had never been an athletic swimmer, but how hard could it be? Boy, was I in for the surprise of a lifetime.

Swimming is hard cardio, and after a few practices, the coach pulled me aside for a chat. "Vlada, you're not exactly varsity swim team material," he stated, trying to be as kind as possible. I felt pathetic and embarrassed, especially since my boyfriend was there and already knew what the coach was about to tell me. I felt shut out and victimized; however, I immediately realized I was no victim. Every one of those swimmers started somewhere, and so would I.

"Coach, I can get there. Give me a shot and let me come and practice every day," I said.

He smiled and said, "You can come practice anytime you want. You're always welcome. Let's see how you do."

Four days a week, at five o'clock in the morning, I was at practice. I was in it to win it. Even as a teenager, I realized I could be a loser who couldn't get on the swim team, or I could be a winner who trained hard to make the varsity team. I wasn't going to turn around and tell everyone I couldn't make the team.

During those few months, I became disciplined and empowered myself by training hard. The coach approached me one day and said, "I can't believe you're still here."

"Coach, I'm here until I make it," I replied. That day, I found out I was allowed on the varsity team, even though tryouts had ended months earlier. I worked my way in, and instead of feeling like a victim as I had three months prior, I was a winner, part of a team, swimming at competitions all over the state, and even winning top placements at swim meets in breaststroke, my best stroke.

I was so confident in myself and my success on the swim team that I tried out for the golf team, despite never having played golf. Another embarrassment awaited as I arrived for tryouts with my neighbor's borrowed golf clubs, wearing jeans and slide-on shoes. The golf coach was appalled by my outfit.

I still don't know how, but I did fairly well in tryouts. I loved the country club environment and seeing a glimpse of the preppy kids' world. The golf team had a junior varsity squad, and I felt I had a great chance. Coach Jordan must have seen something in me because he gave me a spot on the junior varsity team under one condition: I had to buy proper golf shoes and clothes. All the preppy varsity kids picked at me, but I wouldn't be a victim. I would prove myself.

That week, I bought golf shoes and new clubs, and I showed up at the country club, where the team played nine holes every day. I got better and better, and it became noticeable when the hot guy on the team started complimenting me. They showed up in their new cars, while I pulled up in an old 1995 Mitsubishi Galant. And while they worked on their swings with their trainers, I hit golf balls at the driving range alone. I already knew the play—I had to empower myself for success.

Eventually, I made the varsity team. I played in the state tournament and won a small medal in my category. It felt extra special because I was the only team member to win anything. I began as the girl in jeans and ended up becoming the girl in leather European golf shoes, walking out of the tournament with a medal around her neck. Victim to victor—that was me. I never took "no" for an answer, and I never allowed myself to be a victim, so neither should you.

Remove the victim mentality and do something about it by empowering yourself. Stop avoiding accountability and blaming others for the fact that you're a loser in certain situations. You don't have to be a loser; you can be a winner if you do the work. Get past the obstacles. I'm grateful to have learned this at a young age. In every situation I face, I remember the girl who couldn't make the golf team or the swim team, and the girl who chose not to be the victim. I try to make her proud, even today.

CHAPTER NINE LESSONS

Perseverance and resilience are important in the face of rejection. Accepting "no" can hinder personal growth and success, while viewing "no" as a stepping stone can lead to greater opportunities.

1. Rejecting Defeat
Accepting "no" signifies giving up. Not pushing past "no" limits your potential and growth.

2. Changing Your Perspective on "No"
View "no" as a starting point for dialogue and negotiation rather than a final answer. "No" can signal opportunities for re-evaluation and improvement.

3. Identifying the Right People to Ask
Choosing the right individuals to seek help is crucial. Asking someone likely to say "yes" is more strategic than targeting an expert who may not be supportive.

4. Facing the Fear of "No"
Fear of rejection can paralyze personal growth. Overcome these fears by asking confidently and recognizing the benefits of trying. You have more to gain by trying than by missing the opportunity.

5. Empowerment Over Victimhood

Do not adopt a victim mentality when faced with rejection. Instead, take responsibility for your successes and failures and focus on solutions rather than problems.

Embracing a proactive attitude and rejecting defeat leads to personal empowerment and success. By removing the victim mentality and persistently seeking opportunities, you can navigate challenges more effectively and achieve your goals. Always strive for a "yes" rather than accepting a "no."

CHAPTER NINE EXERCISE

Identifying the Fear of No

List ten things you are afraid of going for because you fear rejection:

Start with one at a time.

Make the ask by:
1. targeting the right person,
2. prepping the landscape before you ask by gauging how those individuals feel about the subject,
3. plan to approach them privately.

A "no" now doesn't mean a "no" forever. If you get a "no," build a bridge by finding a pathway and asking what you can work on to get there.

Keep going down your list, one by one.

CHAPTER 10

ALL IS FAIR IN LOVE AND WAR

The single most important decision you can make is who to spend your life with. They can be the paradise of your life or the living hell you constantly have to deal with. They can fill you with life, love, energy, and motivation, or they can drain you, making you anxious, unhappy, and depressed, so choose wisely. Having the wrong partner will destroy your happiness, leave you depleted, and force you to carry the weight of everything alone.

Having the wrong person in your life makes success exponentially more difficult, even if it's someone you're dating for the long run. If the choice is between an unsupportive partner or no partner at all, trust me—you're better off with no one at all. The right partner may not be the wildest, most excitable one, but they will be supportive, stable, and dedicated.

In every chapter of your life, you'll encounter someone new. When you date someone who isn't conducive to your success, they'll be someone you hate and regret later on. They'll bring heartbreak and disappointment because staying with them betrays your dreams, and you'll never forgive them for being the reason you sacrificed or delayed fulfilling those dreams. The right partner must match and enhance your life, not take away from it. Never betray your dreams for someone else.

The partner you consider for marriage must go even further—they cannot be a temporary fit for one chapter of your life. They must align with the big vision you created for yourself. If you can envision them getting you to your end goal faster while providing you with a never-ending cushion of support and motivation, then they are the right fit for you.

While working at the bar in college, I met a Swedish hockey player who played for the National Hockey League team in my state. I didn't realize who he was at first, but I knew he was different. He was hanging outside the bar waiting for his friends when I approached him. "You don't like it inside?" I asked, making small talk.

He looked at me and said, "No, a bar really isn't my kind of place." He was certainly different.

"It's not mine either," I said, and got him a bottle of water as he waited for his friends. As they left, I thought I recognized his friends. As I turned around to return to work, I felt a tap on my shoulder. His friend had returned and asked for my number, saying it was for his friend, Elias, who was too shy to ask for it himself.

I gave him my number, and Elias messaged me within minutes. We texted mostly about awkward bar environments. He always seemed to make me laugh, and his sense of humor was refreshing. He just seemed different. Our first date was after one of his hockey games. He'd made arrangements with a French restaurant to stay open late just for the two of us. The whirlwind romance had begun.

We spent enormous amounts of time together and grew close relatively quickly. I loved cooking in his penthouse kitchen and meeting his friends and family as they visited from Sweden. He hated it when I worked on weekends, but I had no choice. He was in love with me, and I was infatuated with him. My world revolved around him. I was part of the support crew—the loyal girlfriend and his comfort when he got home from away games. It was all about his career. There was never any talk of my goals or aspirations. He didn't seem interested.

Maybe some women love the idea of just being someone's support staff, but it always ends badly. Men quickly lose interest in you when you lose your sense of independence. Trust me on this.

We never discussed my dreams, and he never asked me what I wanted out of life. I wanted to succeed on my own terms, not by marrying a wealthy athlete and living through his dreams. The winter Olympics came that year, and he was playing for the Swedish National Hockey team at the winter games. While immensely proud of his success, I couldn't help but wonder what he'd do next. I initiated many conversations about how he envisioned life after hockey, and his dream was a quiet life in Sweden, which didn't quite match my vision.

He suffered multiple hockey injuries the following year, which took a heavy toll on him. Before I knew it, I faced a tough choice. The hockey team was being sold to Canada, and he asked me if I would move. It would have meant transferring to a university in Canada, and that wasn't where my dreams were.

I realized he only fit into one phase of my life, rather than the big picture, so I had to let him go. It wasn't easy, but deep down, I knew I couldn't betray myself and my dreams. I couldn't be someone's support staff for life. I struggled with the decision, but in the end, I knew he wasn't the one, and changing my entire life to revolve around him wouldn't make me happy.

This is a perfect example of why a good person stays in your life for only one season. He fit nicely into my life for a while, but our relationship came with an expiration date. We enjoyed each other's time and company, and he took nothing away from my life, but in the end, I couldn't sacrifice my future for him.

You'll have people in your life for a season, and if they fulfill you for that time, enjoy it, learn from it, and embrace the beauty of the season. But when the time comes, let them go. Your destinies didn't align for a reason. You have bigger dreams to pursue.

I. VALUE YOURSELF

First and foremost, you can't even begin to think about being in a relationship with someone if you don't value yourself. Even if you're currently in a relationship, working on your self-worth will still benefit and help you get more out of that relationship in the long run. Self-worth is the evaluation of yourself as a capable and valuable human being deserving of consideration and respect. It's your internal belief that you're worthy of love. Greater self-worth leads to greater confidence and naturally higher self-esteem.

To understand your own self-worth, you need to ask yourself:
- Are you happy with yourself?
- Do you think of yourself negatively or positively?

If you think of yourself negatively, that generally signals the start of a journey toward being happy with yourself. Many factors go into deciding if you're happy with yourself. It starts with your values. Being grounded by something bigger than yourself and having a higher purpose is vital for self-worth. How you see yourself everyday matters. Begin by imagining yourself being good at anything you try. Even if it's not true, it doesn't matter—you must believe in yourself when no one else does. I always forced myself to believe I could be good at anything that I put my mind to if I just tried. No one can believe in you until you believe in yourself.

We tie our self-worth to many other factors, but they shouldn't define us. We often tie self-worth to our finances or careers, but self-worth is much more than that. It's knowing you have what it takes inside, regardless of whether you have money or a career.

We also tie self-worth to our social status, which is also a mistake. Who cares what your social status is? I was a poor immigrant, but inside I was a tough cookie, and I wouldn't let anyone define me. I knew I had everything in me that I needed to be successful, and that belief led me to achieve success. If I lost everything today, I could do it all over again because I didn't tie my self-worth to any of those external factors.

Our sense of self-worth is also tied to beauty and appearance. While things don't define you, it certainly doesn't hurt to get your act together and start focusing on making yourself feel beautiful. Buy the nice perfume, commit to the hard workout, and spoil yourself from time to time. Invest in yourself. No one ever suffered from physically looking and feeling better. It will only boost your self-esteem and self-worth. If you're currently in a state where you're not happy with yourself, then you must work on getting to a place where you are, and that starts with self-love. Fall in love with yourself and the parts of you that you can't change.

I always felt that I had self-love and self-worth. I never disliked myself or struggled with self-esteem issues. Imposter syndrome was my only challenge, and I overcame that with time. I once found myself in a horrible and abusive relationship—the only one I have ever had in my life. I realized I had to work on myself so I would never end up in that situation again. Struggling even a little bit with your self-worth can lead to horrible relationships.

Prior to my professional hockey player love interest, I dated someone who was nothing short of a narcissist, and a physically abusive one at that. I had met Tim when I was out with friends for happy hour. He seemed decent, professional, and fairly nice. We began dating, and he continued to be rather charming; however, red flags accompanied the love bombing early on. Unfortunately, I wasn't equipped to recognize them.

They manifested in excessive compliments, grand trips, and discussions about commitment early in the relationship. I had only been in one serious relationship before, so this didn't seem strange at first. It just seemed like he cared for me deeply.

He always wanted to spend time together, which I couldn't manage because of my busy work and school schedule. The more distant I became, the more aggressive he became. He grew possessive, went through my phone, stalked me, and showed up when I was at dinners with friends, and eventually he got violent. It started with light pushing when we fought, but it progressed to name-calling and much worse. I didn't deserve such treatment; I knew my self-worth, but abusive cycles are hard to break. We broke up and got back together multiple times. My friends didn't want to hear about it anymore because they were sick of the toxic cycle with him.

Eventually, he showed up at my job and dragged me out of the building, pushing me into his car. He got physically abusive, and I ran from his house to the police station, which wasn't far away. That day, I broke the pattern, and was left questioning how I'd let it happen. The answer was somewhere deep down—perhaps I doubted my self-worth. Leaving an abuser isn't easy, and no one around you can understand that, in some strange way, you even miss them until you reach the point of healing. It's a complex psychological game.

I dug into my core and worked on myself. My self-worth needed a pick-me-up after that unpleasant situation. For months after the breakup, he continued to reach out, insulting me profusely and attacking my image and character; however, I had built myself up to a point that his words didn't affect me. When you starve a narcissist of attention, they suffocate. That relationship, as horrible as it was, proved how strong I was. I wish I had felt that confidence at the beginning because it might have prevented the relationship from going as far as it did.

This is why the lesson of self-worth is so important to understand. If you don't work on your self-worth, you'll end up in the hands of someone who will capitalize on your weakness, and it'll be difficult to break away. Self-worth comes from loving yourself first, and then the rest will follow.

II. WHAT TO LOOK FOR IN A PARTNER

The biggest danger in relationships is entering them without knowing what you're looking for. If you don't know what you want in a partner, you'll end up playing the trial-and-error game of relationships, and you don't have time for that. Plus, they only end in heartbreak and disappointment—much of which could be avoided if you had just learned what to look for.

Stability is the key building block of a well-rounded individual. The person you date needs to have a stable foundation. Assess how deep their purpose is and how stable their emotions, finances, and social circle are. You'll find that most people drop off the list after you assess their stability. Once someone shows you that they're hyper-emotional, possessive, or quick to anger, they've proven their instability. If their social circle seems toxic and unstable, or they move from circle to circle, that indicates instability. If they mismanage their finances or try to touch your money, they cannot be stable.

The most obvious of these stability factors is purpose. If you find yourself on a date with someone who can't tell you what they're working toward in life, what drives them, or what their dreams and ambitions are, you can easily deduct that they don't have strong roots.

One crucial life lesson is that you cannot change someone. While you can help someone understand you better and adapt to your likes and dislikes, you cannot change their core identity. The faster you realize and accept this, the better off you'll be. Accepting that you can't change someone means you need to understand someone's values and core beliefs upfront and ensure they match what you're looking for. If religion is an important part of your core belief system, make sure you're dating someone who shares your religious beliefs. If marriage is a serious goal, it's essential to align your views on finances, politics, and having kids, too.

Respect is another key attribute to look for in a partner. Their ability to respect you will dictate how they treat you. A man who respects you will always be a gentleman; he will open doors for you, carry your bags, and bring you flowers. A man who sits you on a pedestal will naturally want to help you, do things for you, and treat you with kindness.

If you make it past the last three checkpoints of assessing stability, common values, and respect, then only one detrimental point remains: communication. If you cannot engage in a healthy and productive dialogue with someone, there's nothing more to establish in the relationship. Communication is one of the key ingredients of long-lasting partnerships. Someone who cannot be open to listening to you and actively shuts you down on dates will never make progress in a relationship with you. If they cannot find a healthy way to share their concerns and listen to yours, they are not relationship material.

Stability, common values, respect, and communication are essential attributes to seek in a potential partner. It takes a few dates before you get to know how someone aligns with these attributes; however, paying attention from the beginning will reveal potential, or lack thereof.

Through a mutual friend, I met a great guy who wanted to date me. He coordinated an amazing first date at an Italian restaurant on the other side of town, and it was absolutely the quintessential date spot. He picked me up and was a perfect gentleman, which impressed me. After we ordered some wine and appetizers, he shared his background, and it became very clear that he was very devout in his Catholic faith. I had no issue with that, but

I wasn't Catholic, so I knew right then that he wasn't ideal for the long run. He was also a member of the Freemasons and very dedicated to it, which further highlighted our differing core values.

He was a great, stable guy and met many criteria, but I had to be honest with myself: eventually, we would not see eye to eye on things that mattered in a long-term relationship. After dinner, he invited me to his place to have wine and dessert on his patio. As difficult and uncomfortable as it was, I had to be forthright and tell him I didn't feel it was fair to waste his time because I didn't see a future between us. He was truly devastated, but by being honest, I created space for something more suitable for us. He met an amazing Catholic girl, married her, and started a family, and I moved on to date someone with whom I was much more aligned.

Knowing what to look for in a partner saves you a lot of time and energy. You create the space for an opportunity to meet the right person rather than someone who will only work out in the short term. Many times, I had to cut someone off after a first date. While many didn't appreciate my straightforward approach, it saved us both the headache that would have come later. Do not be afraid to be honest with yourself. You're not here to waste time; you're here to get the most out of life, and in dating, that starts with knowing exactly what you want.

III. THE DATING GAME

The most fun thing we can talk about is the dating game. I can assure you that you're probably doing it all wrong. Think of dating as the Hunger Games, and you're in charge. Only the strong survive in this game. By the time you're actively dating, you've already worked on your self-worth, identified what to look for in a partner, and hopefully worked on your appearance a bit, too. These things set you up to feel your best and be your smartest self.

The best way to meet someone is *not* online. While there have been some success stories, dating online is like a buffet—you have everyone on display. Women tend to narrow down what suits them best, but men fall back on the dating website buffet to look for the next best thing. It's a big dopamine hit for them, especially for those who have never had such access to so many women in their lives.

The best place to meet people is through networking or social events. Put yourself out there where the type of person you're looking for is likely to be. You have the chance to interact with people directly, making it easier to filter out those who don't align or click with you. Get in the habit of being social and putting yourself out there.

Should you disregard my advice and proceed online, treat that venture like a business with a well-defined strategy. Vet anyone you meet online via video call first. There's no need to waste time on coffee until they pass your initial filter. Many will fall off at this stage. If they make it, look through their social media, Google their name, and get to know who you're talking to. Under no circumstances should you disclose that you vetted them. This is for your knowledge only and protects you from ending up with an unsavory character.

When you begin dating, you never date one person at a time. Your dating life should operate on a revolving cycle of going out on dates and getting to know multiple people until you find someone you want to get to know more intimately. Only then do you pause the dating scene and dig deeper. Keep busy, as being "too available" is never appealing to men. Unless there's a direct commitment to being exclusive, don't allow yourself to be played by being the only one who is committed.

You'll only get to know someone deeper after the three-month mark. This tends to be when people start to show their true selves. Often, men will drop off at this stage because red flags appear. Never delay the inevitable—if it isn't feeling right at any point, cut it off immediately. Time is something you can never get back, so don't feel the need to apologize to anyone.

A man needs to provide support, protection, leadership, and clarity—not confusion, questions, and chaos. If at any point you're feeling uncertain or confused, that's your sign to move on. The right man will always treat you with respect. He won't ghost you or turn to cheap manipulation tactics to get your attention. He'll be patient, listen, and always run after you.

Your job is to never chase after a man or put his needs above your own. You must always come first; you are the number one priority. The minute you change this dynamic and start catering to a man around the clock, he'll begin looking at other women. You'll become boring to him because he'll lose the thrill of the chase. Men crave excitement and the pursuit; it's in their DNA. When you become too stable and convenient, giving away too much time and attention, you'll become yesterday's news.

Keep up your intrigue by looking your best, prioritizing yourself and your needs, and never giving up your independence. Losing your freedom is one of the worst things that can happen. A lack of independence signals to a man that you'll always be around because you have no choice. Always be independent enough to leave whenever you please. This alone will keep him begging at your feet.

Feminine energy is important, but career-driven women often find themselves in a masculine mindset—focused on the hustle, bustle, and grind—losing touch with their feminine side. This is a balance I have always prioritized. In your career, you can be as masculine and tough as you need to be, but when dating or committing to someone, you need to channel your feminine energy. Submit and let a man plan the dates, open the doors, and buy you flowers and gifts. Learn to receive love and attention without taking charge, give him the space to be the man he needs to be.

It's important to dress femininely, opting for dresses, skirts, and heels rather than tough pantsuits or casual jeans and sneakers. Give your date the space to lead and take charge. If he fails, makes you split the bill, or can't make the dinner reservation, then he's most certainly not for you.

My Golden Rules for a Date

1. Never split the bill—if a man asks you to split the bill, he is out.
2. Never have more than two drinks on a date.
3. Never wear pants on a first date; being feminine is key, so stick to skirts or dresses.
4. Never have intimate relations with someone without commitment.
5. Never open your own door.
6. Never share anything negative about yourself, especially past trauma.
7. Never over-compliment your date.
8. Never talk more than you listen.
9. Never have bad etiquette.
10. Never use foul language, even in jokes.

My rules for a date have never led me astray. My strategy for filtering out the wrong people has saved me a great deal of time and energy in the dating game. I have always prioritized and respected myself, and it has served me well.

I was well into my career when I met a charming doctor who seemed like Mr. Perfect. He was incredibly good-looking, fit, intelligent, and well-educated. It was clear that he also knew the dating game well. After all, how does someone like him stay single for so long? He had never been married and had no kids, which seemed strange. I added him to my dating rotation, and he quickly became a favorite.

One day, as we were having dinner, he asked if I was seeing other people. I said that I was going on dates until I knew there was a commitment. He said I should stop dating other people, so I asked if he wanted to date more exclusively; however, he couldn't give me a straightforward answer. What was evident was he wanted me to date him exclusively, but it didn't seem like he was committing to that in return.

That dating game continued, but I filtered him out when it became clear that he just wanted a one-sided commitment. One evening after drinks, he tried to take me home with him. I explained that I don't engage in intimacy with someone who is dating around and playing the field. Again, he couldn't deny it and didn't offer any alternative. My boundaries were clear, but he tried to persuade me otherwise by saying that most women don't care, and with time, we'd know if it would work out. After shamelessly flirting with him and leading him on, I left and never saw him again. I knew he would waste my time.

For years, he continued reaching out to me. It may come as no surprise, but he never got married. He remained a bachelor doctor for life. Many women fell for his charm, charisma, and stable career, but I knew better. While the situation was tempting, and I had hoped he would magically be different after a few dates, he wasn't. By cutting off our relationship at the right moment, I saved myself a great deal of time.

Years later, I met a woman who had also known him. She shared how she had wasted two years of her life being intimate with him, despite him never really committing. I felt genuinely sorry for her. She had wasted those peak years only to accept what she saw in him during the first few dates.

All is fair in love and war, so play the game accordingly. You get better and wiser at the game over time. The bad relationships we all experience prepare us for something much better and help us identify what we don't want. Bad partners can lead you down paths that force you to forget your dreams—never let that happen. Stay focused, intentional, and calculating, and you'll find someone who supports all your hopes, dreams, and ambitions. There is no other way.

CHAPTER TEN LESSONS

A life partner will dictate your happiness and the direction of your future. Carefully consider who you allow into your life, as they can affect your emotional well-being and success.

1. Importance of Partner Selection
The right partner can enhance your life, provide support, and motivate you, while the wrong one can drain you. A supportive partner is more crucial than simply being a romantic partner.

2. Seasonal Partners
Some relationships are meant to be temporary, serving their purpose during just one phase of your life. It's essential to recognize when a partner is no longer aligning with your goals and to let them go before they hinder your growth.

3. Self-Worth
You should have a strong sense of self-worth before starting a relationship. Recognize your value, be happy with yourself, and believe in your capabilities. Self-worth should not be tied to external factors like finances or appearances.

4. Red Flags in Relationships

Unhealthy relationships can stem from low self-worth. Recognize and address unhealthy patterns, like manipulation and emotional abuse, to avoid detrimental partnerships.

5. What to Look for in a Partner

Stability, common values, respect, and effective communication are vital traits. Knowing what you want helps avoid wasting time with trial-and-error dating.

6. The Dating Game

Effective dating involves being proactive rather than reactive. Meeting potential partners in social settings rather than online is recommended. Vet potential partners before committing to dates.

7. Maintaining Independence

Independence is paramount. Do not prioritize a partner's needs over your own; you cannot pour from an empty cup. Always maintain your individuality and freedom in a relationship.

8. Feminine Energy

In dating scenarios, embrace your feminine side by allowing men to lead and treat you with care. Focus on qualities that make you glow and draw positive attention. Don't plan dates, make reservations, or try to take charge. These are not feminine traits. Let the man do his part.

9. Date Rules

Establish clear guidelines for dating, such as not splitting bills, maintaining good etiquette, and prioritizing your comfort. These rules help filter out unsuitable partners.

Being intentional in love and dating shapes your path to finding the right partner. By focusing on your self-worth and clearly understanding what you want in a partner, you can navigate relationships that align with your goals and ambitions. This journey ultimately leads to a supportive partnership that enhances your life rather than hinders it. Stay proactive and prioritize yourself, and you will attract the right people.

CHAPTER 11

STOP MAKING EASY DECISIONS

Life is full of decisions, and we often get swept away by where the wind blows, not being intentional about the decisions we make. We don't give them enough thought and end up choosing the simple path, making decisions that seem easier and more sensible in the moment. However, this makes things much harder in the long run. Easy decisions are only easier in the short run, but they ultimately inhibit our ability to achieve the success and growth we seek. The path less traveled is often the more rewarding one in every aspect of success.

Choosing easier options provides short-lived relief and a fleeting sense of success, but in the long run, we are left with regret. Easy decisions rarely align with our goals. They keep you in your comfort zone, and I don't think I need to tell you again that growth doesn't happen within your comfort zone. When you envision something and plan how you'll get there, choosing Easy Street likely won't lead to your end goal. Like it or not, this is another hard truth you must face.

My entire life has been built on making hard choices, not because I wanted to, but because I rarely had a choice. In the short term, some of those hard decisions left me feeling as if I were drowning, but looking back, I see how they set me up for ultimate success.

When I started college, all my high school friends remained in the small town we grew up in. Many of them attended the local community college and started families at young ages. I could have done the same, but it felt restrictive. I wanted to explore beyond my comfort zone, so I applied to a state university in a bigger city. Making the move from a small town with a two-lane highway to a city with seven-lane highways, skyscrapers, and overpriced rent certainly wasn't the easiest choice.

Most of my friends back home had parents to help pay for school, and the ones who didn't applied for student loans. Working during all four years of college to pay for school wasn't easy either. I can't express how hard it was to work sixty-hour weeks while attending school full time. I had to work at a bar because that's where the money was. During the week, I worked daytime shifts in the office after class, and on weekends, I was the nightshift manager. It was grueling being on my feet all weekend, every weekend.

While my friends were all out at college parties or bars, I was working in one. They all bought new cars with their college loan money, and I made monthly car payments and sent money back home to Ukraine to help my grandparents with medical expenses. From the sidelines, it looked like I had a fun college job at a bar, but I was exhausted from balancing full-time school with a demanding work schedule. I was constantly getting sick because my body couldn't handle the lack of sleep and grueling schedule, but I never stopped, never caved in, and never hit the easy button.

The day I graduated and sat in the large Georgia Dome, I cried throughout the commencement speech about taking the path less traveled and blazing your own trail. That was exactly what I had already done and would continue to do. I wouldn't realize the results of those hard decisions until years later.

From that day forward, I began building wealth. Unlike many of my peers, I avoided accumulating six-figure debt. This clean start made a lifetime of difference. Fifteen years later, my friend called to tell me how excited she was to have paid off her college debt. The funny thing about that phone call was the memory of offering her a job at the bar I worked at. She came a few nights but hated it, claiming it exhausted her. The cold, hard truth was that she didn't want to make the hard decision to work. I hated it too, but I knew what I had to do to achieve my goals. I didn't have all the answers back then, but I understood the importance of making hard decisions.

Years later, when I went to Harvard to complete my master's degree, I paid for my education out of pocket to avoid taking out a loan. By then, I knew that if I wanted to stay ahead, that was the only way to do it.

I. TAKING THE RISK

Making tough decisions upfront always feels like a huge risk. Not everyone is eager to take a risk without really understanding the outcome. This hesitation stems from a fear of the unknown and an even greater fear of failure. Making a hard decision means having "blind faith" that it will eventually work out. This is nerve-wracking because it feels like you have no control over a situation, creating a vicious cycle that discourages you from taking risks. In reality, making tough choices gives you the exact opposite: all the control.

Often, we find ourselves weighed down by the opinion of others, which leads to hesitation when it comes to taking risks. There's an unstated pressure to conform, but rest assured, you do not need to meet anyone's standards. Their standards don't have to match yours. People don't grow at the same pace, so their mentality may be limited or narrow-minded. As you start to consider taking risks, they will be the first to tell you it can't be done because, for them, it can't. You are not them—so take the leap of faith. The higher the risk, the higher the reward.

The naysayers who tried to talk you out of it will be the first to applaud you when you reach the finish line, claiming they always believed in you. Unfortunately, that's not true. How could they have believed in you if they couldn't believe in themselves?

When my fiancé and I were on a trip to Ukraine, he became incredibly sick. It was the end of the first year of the COVID-19 pandemic, so we couldn't travel while he was in such an immunocompromised state—not to mention people still needed a COVID test to travel at that time. A colleague of mine informed me of an amazing opportunity six days from then: a trip with a delegation visiting eight African countries with seven heads of state. I understood the value of the opportunity, but I also knew I hadn't been randomly selected to participate. Someone in one of those countries wanted to meet with me.

I asked the question directly. There was a pause on the other end of the line. It was a warlord who wanted to meet with me. I was a bit puzzled—this was new territory, even for me.

Taking part would mean taking personal security risks and potentially damaging my reputation. My fiancé was less than pleased with my desire to fly halfway across the world to meet a warlord. He was extremely sick with COVID and wasn't getting better. I spoke to a contact in my professional network who also expressed concern that it was too risky.

Deep down, I knew high risk often yields high reward. No one understood me, but I knew I had to go on the trip. I packed my bags and was off on an adventure of a lifetime. The trip was incredible. I met some presidents I had never met before. After six days and twelve COVID tests, I finally met the warlord. He was shrouded in mystery, as expected, but to me, he was just a guy with more guns than the other guys.

Still, to this day, I believe that was one of the greatest meetings I have ever had. A five-foot-four blonde in a black suit with no security walked in and broke bread with someone who was the complete opposite. He wanted peace—was that so wrong? If there was a way to help facilitate that, why be afraid? That trip reminds me that making the hard, uncomfortable decisions and taking risks can open doors to unimaginable opportunities. In the end, my fiancé survived COVID, and my risk paid off.

II. EMBRACE THE CHALLENGE

Part of making hard decisions is embracing the challenge. No one wants to face unnecessary challenges, but what no one is telling you is that life is challenging, no matter what. You get to choose your level of hard. It's better to do hard, challenging things voluntarily so you can grow before life forces you to suffer. Lean into the challenge, face the obstacle, and attack it head-on. You cannot grow if you're constantly avoiding challenging situations.

Life is hard no matter how you look at it, so choose your hard carefully. You can be in the best shape of your life or you can be fat, but both are hard in their own ways. You can borrow money from friends or run your own business, working around the clock, but both options have challenges. Prepare yourself for them.

You can overcome your unpreparedness by tackling the challenge directly and accepting that what you're about to sign up for is indeed difficult. Tell yourself that the challenging stage is only temporary and that you have all the skills needed to overcome the challenge. Remember, your skills are your biggest asset, and even your negative qualities, like being overly aggressive, can serve you well in challenging situations.

I was working on a case in Eastern Europe with the United States government, lobbying for an American company that had fallen victim to horrible corruption. It wasn't going to be an easy case. Corruption reached the highest levels of government in that country. The potential for being in danger was very real. If I didn't embrace the challenge, I'd have been choosing the easy way out. Staying in my comfort zone on projects is not my *modus operandi*. I also had a deep purpose in that case, fighting for what I knew was right.

During multiple trips to the country, I was being followed and deliberately intimidated by the authorities. They wanted me to drop the case and get out. The more they played intimidation games with me and my colleagues, the more I doubled down on my position. The only way forward was to attack it head-on.

During a meeting with the authorities, I looked directly across the table at a senior member of the government and said, "Are you done sending your C-level crew to follow me around? Because if that's the best you have, you're in trouble, my friend." He was shocked that I had made a joke of the situation and challenged him in front of his people.

The next time I entered the country, they tried to create issues at the border, but I had enough contacts of my own that I easily gained entry. It became a game for me. I dropped texts to the people targeting me and said, "Better luck next time, friend."

They went so far as to leak false information to a well-known journalist, accusing me of being an agent of propaganda in their country, but I thwarted their attacks until they finally called a truce. Their agents disappeared because they knew I was up for their challenge.

That case was deeply personal to me, and what they were doing was wrong. I had uncovered corruption at every turn, and if I hadn't taken on the fight, it would have only emboldened them to continue doing the same to other American companies.

When you embrace a challenge, you test yourself and discover what you're truly made of. Although I was confident in my abilities before taking on that challenging project, I discovered even more how resilient I was.

In the end, I built a strong network of support for the project and a reputation for working on the most challenging cases, which opened many doors for me. I gained a great deal from tackling the challenge and making the hard decision upfront, and you can, too. Don't shy away from it. Embrace the hard.

III. LONG-TERM IMPACTS

You may feel unprepared to make a hard decision because you can't see far enough to understand the long-term impacts. Let me simplify it for you: easy decisions will be harder in the long term. While you may not fully understand exactly what a hard choice will yield, I promise it will position you further ahead over time. In these situations, you must learn to be realistic.

When something isn't likely to serve you well in the long run, drop it and move on. You'll know it's time to drop something because a fork will appear in the road, and you'll feel puzzled, knowing that one side leads to a great opportunity down the road, but the other side promises something good in the short run only. That is your defining moment: too often, you've chosen what works today rather than what will serve you in the future. Next time, try something different—go for the new opportunity. Yes, that means letting go of what presently works for you in some ways. It's an uncomfortable moment, but it's well worth it. Embrace the fact that, in the long run, it'll work out better than ever.

Accept that whatever the long-term consequence of your decision is, it will pay off. Just because you don't know the exact result doesn't mean you shouldn't make the hard choice. I faced a crossroads that forced me to choose between my personal and professional life. It was one of the hardest decisions I've ever made, but looking back, it was the best one I've made. I seized an opportunity that, at the time, looked like a choice between a career and love, making it impossible to have it all. Eventually, I got it all. I passed the test life threw at me and was rewarded.

On a snowy morning in Washington, DC, I wandered around the monuments, using the time to reflect and think about the company I had just started, but I couldn't get my thoughts in line. I didn't have a solid game plan, but I hoped to secure some projects for the year ahead and enter the field of international political consultancy. As I was standing in front of the Washington Monument, a handsome man with a British accent approached me and asked if I'd take his picture. I kindly obliged. He then offered to return the favor. Although I had dozens of pictures around DC, I agreed. After all, it was beautiful, snowy, and picturesque.

We struck up a conversation and he asked if I knew how to get to the White House. Lucky for him, I was the right person to ask. We continued our chat as we walked, and I told him about my life and political work. He told me about his fascinating life in London as a developer. Before I knew it, we were strolling by the White House and best friends by then. After taking more pictures, we had lunch together, and over the next few days, we became inseparable. A whirlwind international romance had begun.

I drove him to the airport a few days later, and we were both nearly in tears. As the following year went by, we alternated between seeing each other every few weeks in London or the US. We embraced adventure and took fun trips together having the time of our lives. He was the best travel companion. He talked about wanting kids and marriage, and although I wanted it all, I didn't want those things right then. He was a great guy, and we got along incredibly well, but I struggled with the British pub culture. He was always in pubs after work, and I couldn't get used to that cultural norm. I didn't try to change it, but I wondered how it would play out in marriage.

One day, I was offered an incredible project that would require me to travel between the Middle East and Africa, living abroad for the next three to four months. It was a golden opportunity for the professional experience I needed. I thought I could have it all—the relationship and the new project. I vowed to make it work, but as I spent my first month on the project, it became clear I didn't have time to travel to see him. His visits were out of the question due to the confidential nature of my project, and having him stay with me would have made it impossible to hide what I was working on.

I saw a divide in my life—the fork in the road. I had to let something go because they couldn't coexist. My work project was the biggest project I had ever worked on in my career, making it a huge stepping stone in my career. Since I wasn't going to embrace the pub culture anytime soon, and wasn't ready for kids and marriage, I had to let him go.

It sounds easy when you're on the outside looking in, but it gutted me from the inside out. He was the easy, fun, and exciting path, but I had to make the hard choice, knowing I might not find love again anytime soon.

I cried myself to sleep many nights after we agreed to part ways. The distance between us and the weight of the project all became too much to handle. I didn't feel ready for the long-term consequences, nor did I know what the future held. I doubled down on my decision and threw myself into work, finding immense success on my project, which opened the doors to multiple exciting work opportunities.

A year later, I met my future husband—someone who proved that I could have it all. We worked in the same field and he understood what I was working toward. It fit like a glove.

The long-term consequences of my hard decision were incredibly positive. I didn't know at the time of my decision that my story would have a happy ending, and neither will you, but trust that it will. Hard decisions lead to success.

CHAPTER ELEVEN LESSONS

Life is filled with decisions, and we often opt for the easy, short-term solutions without considering the long-term consequences. Although the easy choices may provide immediate relief, they can hinder personal growth.

1. The Impact of Decisions
- Quick and easy decisions often seem appealing but may lead to regret later.
- The more rewarding paths are usually the difficult ones that cause initial discomfort.
- Growth does not occur in comfort zones, and aligning decisions with long-term goals is crucial.

2. Taking Risks
- Making difficult decisions feels risky, as it often involves uncertainty about the outcomes.
- Society's pressures can deter individuals from taking necessary risks.
- Embracing risk can lead to substantial rewards; doubters may eventually support you once you succeed.

3. Embracing Challenges
- Choosing to confront challenges rather than avoiding them helps foster personal growth.

- Life inevitably presents difficulties; it's better to choose hard challenges voluntarily so you can learn and grow.
- Attacking obstacles directly can reveal your true capabilities and build resilience.

4. Long-term Impacts
- Easy decisions may lead to complications down the line, while tough choices can result in better long-term outcomes.
- Identify when something no longer serves you and pursue new opportunities, even at the cost of abandoning current comforts.
- Difficult choices may lead to personal and professional success, even when the future seems uncertain.

Choosing the hard path often leads to greater success and fulfillment. Embrace challenges and risks and recognize their long-term benefits. The journey may be uncomfortable, but making tough decisions ultimately fosters personal and professional growth. Trust in the process; hard choices usually bring rewarding results.

CHAPTER 12

THE TABLE

Having a seat at the table means having the influence and power to shape outcomes in different areas of your life. The table represents the power circle, and chances are you haven't been at the table yet. You don't know why, but I do: it's because they don't want you there. The table doesn't have many seats, and you either haven't proven that you're good enough to be there, or you've proven that you're too good, and they fear you'll flip their entire table upside down.

I've been in both positions, and I've moved tables so many times I eventually built my own table. If you don't know how to secure a seat at the table, that's okay. By the time we're done here, you'll know the table playbook. Maybe the table isn't even on your radar, but it should be.

If you don't fight for a seat, you'll spend your entire life being controlled by someone else's decisions.

As you network and grow your professional powerhouse, you'll realize it takes more than smiles and small talk to keep up. Whether you're in college, have graduated, are in the mid-career phase of your life, or are experiencing a midlife crisis, the same rules apply to you. The tables of power are all around you, and the faster you understand what they are and how to get to them, the better for your journey to success.

The table is the circle that holds the cards. In your social environment, there are three tables: your friend group, your family, and your community. In your work environment, there's a corporate table as well as a resources table that has access to money and investment. Every industry has its table. The legal community, for example, has its power table of lawyers and judges. For you, the most important tables will be your work-oriented table and your influence tables, which drive you to fulfill part of your purpose. Once you identify the table you want to focus on, you need to be smart about your approach.

Playing smart means starting from a distance. When you make a play for the table, no one can know your ambitions—not even your inner circle. It's you versus you. First, you need to identify who's controlling things at work, in your social circles, and in your personal settings. Every one of these circles has its Achilles' heel. The weakest link has a seat at the decision-making table, but they're vulnerable, like prey, and they're the unsuspecting target. Go for this target, but never show your hand. Make friends, learn the rules they play by, and play the perfect idiot for a while. Understand who is who, who controls what, and where they spend their time. Use your newfound contacts to get into events, social gatherings, and rooms where the bigger players play. They'll bring you in willingly because they won't suspect you have such high ambitions. In fact, they'll want to help you, thinking you know nothing and no one. Continue building that trust. Eventually, you'll catch a break. It could be a dinner, an important meeting you wouldn't normally have been a part of, an invitation to collaborate on a project, or a social gathering you've never been invited to. When you get there, you have one job: watch and learn.

Your first entrance into this mix should be carefully played and calculated. They'll test you out and want to take a bite to see what you're made of. Stay humble and prove your value when they approach you. Demonstrate your knowledge to prove that you understand and align with their goals, but do not appear too desperate to prove yourself. These people can smell desperation from a mile away.

As you continue making appearances in their circles and building relationships with others, you open the door to getting invited to more meetings, participating in more projects, and gradually integrating into their comfort zone. Show yourself to be useful and help them solve problems. Confidence is key, and even if you don't feel like you have any, fake it till you make it. Use your voice to demonstrate your intelligence. Imagine it like a performance where you play a character. Learn to speak like them, dress like them, and be the most mature, professional, well-versed version of yourself. None of these people should ever become your closest friends. This is how you fail at the game.

As you continue to understand their needs, stay persistent. You'll get noticed, and that's how you earn an invitation to the table. It may manifest as a promotion, greater inclusion, or in various other forms.

Once you get there, understand that not everyone can stay at the table. It's likely that the weakest link will get the boot. That's okay; you're not there to save anyone—you're there for yourself and your own goals. Nothing else matters, so stay focused. Operate like a woman with a man's mind. It makes you less predictable.

You'll soon realize that you're starting to master the table. You'll get to know all the players and who's useful. Do not attempt to overtake the king of the table until you feel ready. By that point, you may not want to overtake him, but rather switch tables instead. When the table feels easy, it may be time to transition to the next one. For now, remember the rules of the table:

The five B's for the boss you're going to become at the table game:
- Be valuable
- Be persistent
- Be confident
- Be a leader
- Be an initiator

In my world, the table in politics represents government and political movements. I learned the dynamics of the table early in my career when I entered the political world. I made a friend who was heavily involved at the national level of the political party I was working for. I was an outsider without a seat, and yet I didn't even know I should be sitting at a table.

The national level influenced most of the decisions at the state level. The rules of the game quickly became clear. There were two levels: one was the state-level political system, where the head is the chair of the party, and then the state-level leadership included the governor, lieutenant governor, secretary of state, and attorney general. They had their own clique and table—the good old boys' table. Georgia is a southern state, and the southern network runs deep. While I love them dearly, I didn't exactly grow up in that network. I became heavily involved in their state-level circle, attended their events, picked off their weakest links, and got to know the circle well. Space at the table was limited.

When some of them were elected to the federal office, they had to play a different game at the second table, where decision-makers held national power. I quickly found the link between the state-level table and the national one. I immediately planned a visit to Washington, where I sat next to the man I had identified as my link. I approached him for mentorship and advice, appearing unsuspecting. He brought me into the fold, connected me across the national level, and opened doors.

I began showing up everywhere but soon became too visible. They started wondering what I was doing there, so I adjusted my approach and kept my distance, channeling one-on-one meetings with key members of that table instead. I led with confidence and brought value, and while I wasn't sitting at their table daily, I was involved in parallel to it. None of them knew that every single one of them was in contact with me in some way. I knew what was happening at a state level before the members at the first table I'd been a part of knew anything. Through that network, I met some of the top consultants in my field who began bringing me into their projects. Before I knew it, I was visiting the White House, which eventually led me to the international political arena.

I never abused my privilege or crossed anyone, and I maintained my reputation in those circles. I moved so quickly through the system that many didn't realize I was already in the international arena. No one knew how I got there; in fact, I still get asked how I got into working internationally. Just like me, you can navigate your way through the system to benefit yourself. Now that you know the rules, you have no excuse—go find the right table.

I. LEAVING THE TABLE

You've already seen how I navigated from one table to the next, but that was a time in my career when I was still learning the ropes. As I advanced in my career, I gained experience that threatened some people who shared a table with me. To them, I was the wild card; they didn't know what to expect from someone like me. This will happen to you, too. It's a natural part of growth.

The biggest mistake you can make is staying at the same table where you started. Once it serves its purpose, leave and move upward. Outgrowing your table will make you stagnant, preventing any real progress. You'll know when the time is right. It'll feel as if you've outgrown their level of power, contacts, and influence. The same table you once dreamed of sitting at will no longer serve you in the same way.

Before you transition, identify where you want to go next. Leaving a table without a new landing pad isn't wise. Look for the table that can help you level up in life. Always look upward.

Working in the international arena means working with consultants from all over the world. A small circle of them was working closely with wealthy Gulf nations. One of the consultants, Charles, brought my firm into an election for the chairperson of a multinational organization, with one of the Gulf nations putting up their candidate. Our team worked tirelessly to gain support from key Balkan countries for their bid. All countries participated in the vote.

Charles and I forged a great partnership, working on top-secret initiatives. At times, he seemed intimidated by having me at his table because of the senior, experienced people I brought with me. Charles wanted to play kingpin, but my circle challenged that, so I had to play carefully at the table. I noticed multiple attempts to undermine my value and that of the people I brought on board. That was a red flag that I should have paid closer attention to.

I began operating more carefully, but then, at the yearly United Nations Summit in New York, Charles attempted to outplay me. I was there with multiple presidential delegations, and on the way to a meeting, one of the Secret Service agents pulled me aside for a private discussion, which was highly unusual. He informed me that Charles secured a meeting with my client, a president, and had expressed that my team and I should be fired, and offered to take on the work himself. It was a shocking betrayal.

Yes, we were from two different companies, but we worked together often as international power brokers, but Charles had never expressed an interest in working for this president before. I was in shock and decided to message him. When he became avoidant and dismissive, his guilt was apparent. I forgive, but I don't forget.

That week, I walked away with half of the power players from Charles' table, and they never spoke to him again. These were serious people: billionaires, leading consultants, and former ambassadors. The loss would affect him significantly. He broke the rules and played against one of his own. We could have accomplished so much together, but he wanted to erase me instead.

That was the day I realized it was time to build my own table. I addressed the issue directly with the president of the country I was working for, and he told me that the minute he heard Charles was trying to smear my name, he asked his security to alert me. I was honored by the respect he had for me. He went so far as to say that he never wanted to see Charles working in his country. He'd witnessed Charles's true character, and so had I.

This experience taught me a great deal. It was about more than just a paycheck. I intimidated Charles, and he couldn't stand that a woman half his age exuded such confidence and skill, leading to strong business relationships where those engaged with me respected my work and supported me. While I didn't know everything, I had people around me who did, and I was doing more than Charles was by learning how to leverage expertise. Instead of playing on the same team and benefitting from it, his small-mindedness led him to betray me. In the end, he lost half his table and half his influence.

To succeed, you must understand when it's time to build your own table. You're ready once you've learned everything there is to learn from the various circles you've been a part of. Just like Charles, those people aren't necessarily proud of you; they're just dumbfounded when you keep making things happen. Don't be mistaken—they'll be intimidated by you, so get ready to play your own game at your own table. Don't be scared; this is the best part. You're the kingpin, so you set the rules and manage the outcomes. You are the center of power in your own world.

II. BUILDING YOUR OWN TABLE

The concept of building your own table can be scary. It's another unknown. I had no idea how to build my own table, but I knew I had no choice. I was so far along in the game that I became too intimidating to be at other people's tables. When you reach this point, you'll have no idea how to build your own table either, but that doesn't mean you can't learn. Building your own tables gives you the power to create your own opportunities. You'll build your own circle where you'll engage in high-level discussions and make important decisions. Your table will also serve as your advisory board when you need direction. Building it requires intense strategy. Here are some key considerations:

Purpose
What do you need to make you more successful?
- Be clear about your mission and purpose.
- Determine what you want your table to represent and achieve.

Network
Who do you need around you to accomplish your mission?
- Identify the type of people you need at your table.
- Make sure they're like-minded and share your goals and ambitions.
- Look for *partners*. You'll be stronger together, especially if your partners have different strengths.

Diversity
What kind of backgrounds do you need?
- Identify people across different industries.
- Identify people who bring unique cultural perspectives.

After Charles's betrayal, I was forced to go back to the drawing board. That was the first time I didn't have a table to jump to. I needed to recalibrate and realign with myself, my "why," and my vision.

I started with my purpose, and while becoming more successful was a huge part of it, there was more to it. No matter how big or small, I wanted to create change in the world. I aimed to focus my work on making a meaningful impact in developing countries, rather than just developed ones. I wanted to be surrounded by people who also aspired to make life better for others—helping governments not only with good governance but also with food security, poverty alleviation, and better access to healthcare and electricity.

This new vision renewed my motivation and drive. I realized I'd need to surround myself with people who had diverse backgrounds in various industries and the same core values. This would be our common thread. I would build a table for changemakers. I set out on a mission to go through my professional and extended contacts to become part of this new journey. Out of everything I've done in my life, this would become the most valuable endeavor to me.

III. WHO IS ALLOWED AT YOUR TABLE?

Building your own table is one of the most rewarding things you can do. At this point in your life, you have no idea how to start. First, you need to understand that not everyone deserves a place at your table. It's exclusive, and it's meant to serve you. Trust is the foundation of your table. Surround yourself with people who will fight for you when you're not in the room.

You may have a thousand enemies and ill-wishers outside your circle, but having even one in your circle is far worse, so choose wisely. When your table is full of go-getters, changemakers, and fighters, you will go far. Consider inviting mentors, people who challenge you, people in different professional industries, and people from different cultural backgrounds. Diversity is important, so look at situations from all angles, not just from your perspective. This approach will make you more well-rounded, productive, and successful in the long run.

When I built my table, my purpose wasn't only to expand my business and network, but to do things that would bring about change. To build the changemakers' table, I needed to focus on key people who would make it happen, so I started with a practical approach.

I needed a lawyer, so I approached one of my closest friends whom I ended up cofounding a law and consulting firm with. I also needed a trustworthy politician, and a lifelong family friend was a perfect candidate. He had a strong network and was a great strategist. He brought a different perspective, which I needed. Next, I needed a businessperson who was an outside-the-box thinker and worked for change in their part of the world, and I had the perfect candidate—an intelligent and successful friend from Africa. Then I needed someone who understood food security issues, and I approached a good friend from Ukraine who had already helped some developing nations. Lastly, I included a powerful Indian changemaker who had worked in developing countries in the energy sector. He was incredibly successful and humble. These individuals became the founding pillars of my table.

You'll notice a few things about my table. First, I was the least successful person. That was intentional; I wanted to surround myself with people who had done more and experienced more than me. How else could I grow?

Second, I only recruited one inner-circle friend. This was also intentional; do not fill your power table with friends. It never ends well. You can thank me later for the pro tip.

Third, my table is diverse, spanning four continents and featuring people from different backgrounds and industries. It has since grown to include more people.

Fourth, my table doesn't include many women. As hard as it is for me to admit, most women aren't supportive of each other. They're hyper-emotional, quick to become jealous, and bring problems. This is the reality. I always support women, but I rarely find the same in return. Be careful of this. Not all women support women, so look for the rare ones who do.

My table didn't build itself, and neither will yours. I built mine with careful consideration and intention. Always look for accomplished, intelligent, and business-minded individuals. Offer them value, and they'll be inclined to join your table. They may circulate among other tables, but having them on your team will be a significant win that'll get you far.

CHAPTER TWELVE LESSONS

Having a seat at the table means having the influence and power to affect outcomes in various areas of your life. You may not have experience at the tables of power due to being unrecognized or because you intimidate the existing power dynamics.

1. The Table
- The table represents the power circles in your social and professional environments, including family, friend groups, and corporate settings. Each industry has its own tables where decisions and influences happen.

2. Strategic Approach
- To secure a seat, play smart and start by observing from a distance.
- Understand who controls your environment and identify the weakest link in those power structures. This allows you to make calculated moves without revealing your ambitions.

3. Networking and Building Relationships
- Begin building relationships cautiously, showing value in your contributions without appearing desperate.

- Engage in meetings and gatherings where key players interact and aim to solve their problems to demonstrate your usefulness.

4. Integration and Visibility
- The more visible you are in power circles, the greater your opportunities.
- Develop confidence as you interact with key players in these environments.

5. Development Into Leadership
- As you become more integrated into their circles, show confidence and start taking initiative.
- Avoid venturing into personal relationships with the individuals at the table; maintaining a professional distance is crucial.

6. Mastering the Table
Wait to challenge the established leaders until you've got a good grasp of the game and the players involved. If the table becomes too easy, consider moving to a higher table for greater challenge.
- Remember the Five B's for Success. To excel in the game of influence, adopt the following principles: Be valuable, Be persistent, Be confident, Be a leader, and Be an initiator.

7. Moving Up

As you gain experience, know when to leave the tables that no longer serve your growth. Always look for opportunities that facilitate upward movement in your career.

8. Building Your Own Table

- **Defining Purpose:** Be clear about your goals and what you want to achieve collectively.
- **Choosing the Right Network:** Surround yourself with individuals whose ambitions align with yours.
- **Valuing Diversity:** Include people from various backgrounds and industries to enrich discussions and insights.

9. Choosing Who Sits at Your Table

Only trustworthy and capable individuals should be allowed at your table. Establishing your own table can be daunting, but it allows you to create opportunities and direct your path to success. It requires strategic thinking, the ability to leverage relationships, and a commitment to surrounding yourself with accomplished individuals.

CHAPTER 13

DEMAND MORE IN LIFE

We've covered a great deal together so far. Although I've given you the bible of success, I cannot be with you every step of the way. Now you need to take the success mentality with you every day and make it a part of you. Your mind should operate in success mode. What makes success mentality permanent rather than a fleeting phase is your ability to enter a never-ending mode of demanding more. You cannot have more if you don't demand more. It's that simple. Until now, you've only gotten what you've asked for.

Moving forward into a life of success requires you to create a vision, make a plan, set goals, eliminate distractions, and re-evaluate your surroundings to help you gain optimal speed. Above all, it requires you to always demand more. You should never settle.

When I bought my first home, it superseded all my expectations, and yet, less than a year later, I was already looking for my next property. I didn't plan on selling my dream home, but I wanted to own property all around the world. Why have one home when you can have ten? I understood that getting there required hard work, but the point was clear: I was demanding more and would accept nothing less. This continual demand for more pushes you to strive further, and with each passing day, you'll work toward that goal.

I. APPRECIATING YOUR PROGRESS

When you run a million miles a minute, you don't take time to smell the roses. If you don't stop to appreciate your progress, it's hard to find the motivation to move forward. Recognizing your progress and success is motivational and helps you keep moving onward and upward. Stop and reflect on your life's achievements. It's essential to check in with yourself regularly to appreciate all you've done.

As you reach new levels of success, take a moment and step away to relax. Make this a yearly ritual for recalibration, gratitude, and appreciation. Gratitude is crucial for maintaining a success-oriented mindset. It shifts the focus from what you haven't accomplished yet to what you have achieved, mentally preparing you to achieve even more.

Gratitude helps you spot opportunities to learn, grow, and prosper.

People who reflect on their successes tend to have a more positive outlook on life in the long run. When you learn to appreciate what you have, you'll work harder to accomplish new goals. Gratitude helps you evaluate both wins and losses, leading to smarter decision-making in the future.

In my late twenties, I was running so fast I didn't even realize I'd become a millionaire. Sounds bizarre, doesn't it? I was so focused on winning and succeeding that I missed the biggest milestone of an entire decade of my life.

After my thirty-first birthday, I moved into my new house, and that's when it hit me: I was a millionaire. When did that happen? I sat on the stairs of that empty house in silence for half an hour, crying tears of gratitude. That day, I realized the importance of stopping to smell the roses. Life goes by quickly, and while I've urged you to succeed and move at optimal speed, I cannot emphasize the importance of pausing at the end of the year, or after every accomplished goal, to appreciate it.

The following year, I worked ten times harder, realizing I had to triple my success. Despite the COVID-19 pandemic, that year was the most challenging, but it became my most successful year. At the end of the following year, I finally took my own advice and disconnected for the entire month of December. I flew to Dubai and rented a five-star hotel suite for my entire family and me. I indulged in room service almost every day, swam daily, and visited the spa every other day. I used that time to reflect on the last decade of my life.

What's most amazing about this story is that I gifted myself time to appreciate myself and my progress, which opened the door for me to set some serious new goals. The following year, I found myself in my new penthouse in Dubai, with a flourishing property portfolio. Who would have guessed that a year prior to my much-needed time of reflection, I'd be there? Appreciation and gratitude will take you far, so don't take it for granted.

II. SETTING BIGGER GOALS

After taking the time to appreciate how far you've come, it's time to set your next big goal. Always check back in on your big-picture vision. Does it need any adjustments? If so, step up and make the necessary changes. This will help you set the right goals for the next chapter of your life.

The biggest problem I see every day is that people don't set bigger goals. Once they accomplish their primary goal, they get comfortable and are disinclined to reach higher. In order to experience continuous growth and maintain a never-ending success mentality, you must set bigger goals. This forces you to step outside your comfort zone regularly and become more creative in your approaches. The bigger the goal, the more innovative you'll need to be. Think outside the box. There's no other choice. Bigger goals unlock your potential.

As I transitioned into another chapter of success, I recognized that I had to realign my entire vision. My next goal was to get married, which presented the challenge of a lifetime. After accomplishing so much professionally, it was time to get serious about love. This became my next, much bigger goal—one I really wasn't sure how to tackle. Being who I am, you can imagine how I approached the subject of love and finding a life partner. Of course, I applied all my methods and painted a vision of the kind of partner I desired: an intellectual man who was accomplished, kind, and handsome. My standards may appear high, but you've gotten to know me a little, so you know I'm not one to lower my standards.

Unlike my friends who dated losers, I established high standards no loser could meet. No, I did not create some ridiculous checklist. I find that frivolous. Instead, I had a clear idea of what I was looking for: a life partner and marriage. The process of elimination became my favorite tool. I eliminated them one by one, and they dropped like flies.

First, I do not split the bill. An accomplished, decent, and respectful man will never make you split the bill. You either pay the whole bill and never talk to that loser again, or he pays the bill and survives for another round of your hunger games. There are no other options.

If a date can't tell you what happened in World War II, then they're also out. Shallow, unintelligent men will lead you nowhere. You'll lose everything sitting next to a fool, no matter how successful you are.

This bigger goal forced me to assess what I brought to the dating table. I made sure to stay in shape, which is essential for mental and physical well-being. If I couldn't love myself and my body, how could I expect someone else to?

Let's get real: stop this idiotic mantra: "he has to love me for who I am." How can he love you for who you are if you don't even love yourself the way you are? He can't love you for you if he can't see your eyes through the puffiness caused by a horrible diet and poor habits. I became knowledgeable about various subjects and got serious. Meeting a man at a bar or a club was not the way to go. Those places are full of losers pretending to be everything they're not. It works out on rare occasions, but I wanted to stack the odds in my favor.

I attended professional networking events, dressed professionally, yet sexy and femininely, opting for more form-fitting dresses over pantsuits. I learned to flirt, to be charming, and somewhat elusive. Any first date that didn't feel right wasn't worth a second one. This bigger goal was by far the most challenging, but it paid off when I met my future husband.

I had worked with him for some time at the firm I'd merged my company into. He was going through a horrible divorce, and a partner at the firm suggested I go on a date with him. I don't enjoy mixing business and pleasure, so I was hesitant. He was interested, but was I? He certainly met the criteria, but he had kids from his previous marriage, so I wasn't sure. I left it alone for a while, but I eventually gave in.

If I was going to blend my professional and personal lives together, it couldn't be a game. It had to be serious. On the first date, I laid it out clearly: I told him I wasn't dating to kill time; I was looking for something serious. He told me on our first date that, despite his failed marriage, he was serious, too.

After our first date, I never looked back. He was the one. Playing games wasn't his style. He courted me for months like a gentleman and was always on his A-game. He was a winner. Together, over the years, we built an amazing life. I could never have reached that milestone if I hadn't been intentional about wanting more and demanding it.

No matter what your next big goal is—even if it's falling in love—don't hesitate to go for it. If you get stuck, remember to follow the framework for setting goals. You'll get there.

III. LOOKING FOR WHAT'S NEXT

The funny thing about becoming a millionaire in my twenties, finishing a Harvard degree, and building the empire I envisioned is that it made me realize that it didn't take a lifetime to achieve my big-picture vision. I did it in less than ten years. So, what now? It never ceases to amaze me that when I dreamed up my big picture, I had no idea how I would get there. I had no resources, no job, and mere pennies in my bank account. Amazing things can happen when you follow the recipe for success, remove the obstacles in your mind, and free yourself from your own oppression.

The challenge becomes not getting comfortable at this elevated level of success. I wrote this book for you because I want to make success attainable for anyone willing to work for it. Truthfully, I also wrote this book to push myself back out of my comfort zone. I wanted to learn something new, go beyond my own limitations, and serve others. Now that I've come full circle, I, like you, am facing a new big-picture vision. It feels like starting the cycle all over again as a rookie. My new vision—the journey toward a billion—feels unrealistic and scary. I can't help but remember that same feeling I had fifteen years ago.

I remind myself of the young Ukrainian girl who immigrated to the United States with only her mother, two hundred dollars, and a cardboard sign. That little girl deserved more in life, and I will never forget her. She is central to my purpose and pushes me out of every comfort zone I find myself in. I owe it to her and to my mother, who sacrificed so much. There were times when we split a piece of bread for breakfast and walked together in the snow wearing sandals with socks because we had no other shoes. When the going got tough, she never quit. This was all for her. She is my "why."

I share this with you because when you reach what you think is the pinnacle of success, remember that there's always more. The most difficult test comes when you believe you're almost done. In that moment, go back to your "why" and remember that core purpose. Only through this challenge can you push yourself to get to work and start creating the next big plan for your life. In the end, nothing matters but your "why." It's your driving force, your beginning, and your end. Never forget it.

CLOSING

I cannot wait to see what you'll accomplish. Everything you've ever needed can be found deep within you. You possess all the qualities necessary for success. By focusing on what you want, you can create a vision and a plan. Have faith in your ability to have it all, and work toward your goals in small, manageable steps. You'll get there.

Take what I've said seriously, and stop making easy decisions—you'll pay for them later, times ten. Eliminate bad influences from your life, cut out anything that isn't serving you, execute daily, and stay focused. Get used to facing the unknown, the new, and the scary. Never let anyone force you into accepting "no" for an answer. Always demand more from yourself and from life. Do not stop until you get there.

I have given you the things I never had: the tools and the blueprint. You have absolutely no excuse not to emerge as an overwhelming success. Do the work, get the prize, and repeat. You have the recipe, so GET IT DONE! Remember, I'm not going anywhere. I'm waiting to see your finished product, and I won't settle for anything less.

Vlada Galan

CHAPTER THIRTEEN LESSONS

To keep growing, keep setting bigger goals, reflect on progress, and continually demand more from life. Appreciation, gratitude, and your vision are vital for achieving sustained success.

1. Adopting a Success Mentality
- Transitioning to a success mentality requires commitment and consistency.
- To achieve more, you must actively demand more.
- Success is driven by the willingness to push for greater achievements.

2. Appreciating Progress
- To remain motivated, take time to pause and acknowledge your success.
- Regular reflection fosters gratitude and helps you refocus on opportunities for growth.

3. The Role of Gratitude
- Gratitude shifts focus from unmet goals to current achievements.
- This mindset enhances problem-solving and decision-making for future endeavors.

4. Setting Bigger Goals

- After achieving milestones, reassess your vision and set more ambitious goals.
- Continuous growth requires stepping out of comfort zones and thinking creatively.

5. Looking for Next Steps

- Achievements can come faster than expected, but it's essential to keep striving for more.
- Do not become complacent. Continue seeking new challenges and building on your purpose.

6. Rediscovering Purpose

- A clear sense of purpose serves as the driving force behind continual personal and professional growth.

Success is a continuous journey. It's crucial to appreciate achievements while keeping an eye on your future goals. Reflecting on personal growth and maintaining a strong sense of purpose drives ongoing success. Never forget your "why," as it fuels your passion and ambition in life.

Continue Your Path to Success.

Scan and follow the Success Mentality community.

www.ingramcontent.com/pod-product-compliance
Lightning Source LLC
Chambersburg PA
CBHW072150070526
44585CB00015B/1075